Comments on

FROM VENDOR
TO BUSINESS RESOURCE

"*From Vendor to Business Resource* describes the science of selling for the new era, the way *Strategic Selling* described it for the old. This is a must-read inside any company whose business model still includes field salespeople."

Richard L. Flood
President
PSM, MetalTek International

"The concept of salesperson as Business Resource has always been the 'Holy Grail' of selling. It's what all executives want but haven't been able to define. Jerry nails the definition and then shows salespeople how to put it into practice."

Joe Lanzillotta
Vice President, Field Operations
Output Technology Solutions

"Stapleton gets it. With product and pricing information now available at the click of a mouse, the value contribution of salespeople is suddenly called into question. *From Vendor to Business Resource* prepares the sales professional to add value in this new environment."

Mark A. Radtke
President
WPS Energy Services

Transforming the
Sales Force
for the New Era of Selling

From **Vendor**
to **Business**
Resource

Jerry Stapleton

Foreword by Rick Justice
Senior Vice President, Worldwide Field Operations, Cisco Systems

SUMMA
BUSINESS BOOKS

Text Design by Kate Hawley
Cover Design by Shelby Keefe
Edited by Carolyn Kott Washburne and Chris Roerden
Indexed by Carol Roberts

06 05 04 03 02   5 4 3 2 1

ISBN 0-9715445-0-6
Library of Congress Control Number: 2001119697

First Printing 2002

Printed in the United States of America

Originally published by Printstar Business Books
Published by Summa Business Books
1331 Red Cedar Circle, Fort Collins, CO 80524

To Laura,

love of my life,

who held the whole thing together.

Acknowledgments

Writing a book is a humbling experience. I dare say this book would still be a mass of sticky notes had I not been blessed with the support of so many talented professionals. I am especially grateful to Susan Pittelman and the rest of her team at Printstar Business Books: Carolyn Kott Washburne, Kate Hawley, Shelby Keefe, Mike Baldwin, Anne Kaiser, Carol Roberts, and Jeff Grandt, and to Sandy Balzo of Balzo Communications.

Nor would this book exist were it not for the many clients who have entrusted me to represent them as I worked in the trenches alongside *their* salespeople calling on *their* customers. Among these clients, I owe a special debt of gratitude to my friends at: COSS Development Corporation, J.J. Keller & Associates, Schenck AccuRate, Inc., and WPS Energy Services. I'm likewise grateful to the hundreds of salespeople who, independent lone wolves that most of them are, allowed me to join them on calls—often with some of their most prized contacts—so they could learn the countless little things that define the big difference between the salesperson as Problem-Solver and the salesperson as true Business Resource.

Most importantly, I thank my children: Jennifer, Emily, Matthew, Sean, Leah, and Elliott, who have cheerfully endured these past two years with a dad whose time and attention were often unfairly parceled out to their rival "sibling."

Table of Contents

FOREWORD BY RICK JUSTICE xiii

INTRODUCTION. xv

CHAPTER 1
Death of the Vendor 1

CHAPTER 2
Birth of the Business Resource 13

CHAPTER 3
How to Operate in Seek Mode 27

CHAPTER 4
How Organizations *Really* Work 51

CHAPTER 5
Understanding the Customer's Business 73

CHAPTER 6
How to Get to Executives 91

CHAPTER 7
The Business Presentation 123

CHAPTER 8
Pragmatic Positioning 141

CHAPTER 9
Opportunity Assessment 159

CHAPTER 10
From Training to Transformation 179

INDEX 199

List of Figures

FIGURE 2-1   The Customer's Perception of Your Value 14

FIGURE 6-1   Sample Letter: Hooking to an Executive's
              Specific Priorities 111

FIGURE 6-2   Sample Letter: Building on an
              Existing Relationship 113

FIGURE 7-1   Sample Business Presentation
              Pages 1–6 134
              Pages 7–12 135

FIGURE 8-1   Example of Implementing an Indirect
              Method of Engagement in an RFP Response 151

FIGURE 8-2   Example of Implementing an Indirect
              Method of Engagement to Stop a Purchase
              from a Competitor 154

FIGURE 9-1   The Opportunity Assessment Matrix 164

Foreword

I can't think of a company that I admire more than Cisco Systems, especially when it comes to the leadership role they play in the business of selling. Nobody has done more than Cisco to redefine the role of the salesperson away from "order handling and basic information flow" to "value creation for customers."

For example, Cisco's Internet commerce orders account for almost 90 percent of the company's overall sales volume, and more than 80 percent of all customer support questions are answered by a quick visit to Cisco's Web site. Yet their customer satisfaction and retention ratings are legendary.

The use of technology in this way might seem like a threat to the traditional sales force. And it might, indeed, be a threat if Cisco had a traditional sales force. Instead, what this technology does is free up each of Cisco's sales professionals to be the very "Business Resource" referred to in the title of this book. That's why I'm so pleased that Rick Justice, Cisco's Senior Vice President of Worldwide Field Operations—the executive at Cisco responsible for the sales of all Cisco products worldwide—agreed to write the foreword of From Vendor to Business Resource.

—Jerry Stapleton

It's clear that salespeople need to find new ways to cope with and succeed in today's dynamic work environment. Managing an abundance of information, keeping up with new technologies, including the Web, and dealing with a quickly changing global economic landscape are just a few of the challenges facing salespeople today. These challenges are driving a "new era" for selling.

There's no shortage of advice about changing salespeople from "product vendors" to "creators of business value." What's more difficult to find is good advice on *how* to make that evolution happen. *From Vendor to Business Resource* does an excellent job of capturing the essence of the new era's sales model and detailing exactly what it takes to implement that model.

In the past, selling was about delivering information to customers. Today, it's about delivering *value*. Once you deliver value, you move beyond the status of vendor to become a trusted business partner. At Cisco, that's our top priority. We operate in what Stapleton describes as "seek mode," seeking information so that we can better solve customers' business problems. We aim to be a business resource and trusted advisor to our customers. This is what delivers value . . . and ensures short-term and long-term success.

One of the barriers that prevents salespeople in traditional organizations from becoming strategic business advisors is that much of their time is consumed by transactional tasks. At Cisco, we provide our sales team with Web-based tools to handle some of the transactional aspects of selling, such as order handling. This frees up their time so they can focus on the more strategic aspects of selling.

Using the Web to conduct business also makes it easier to do business with Cisco. And, because we're using the very networking technology we sell, we build credibility and reinforce our business resource relationships with customers.

From Vendor to Business Resource is its own valuable business resource. It spells out the actions that organizations—from senior management on down—must take to nurture the new era sales culture and create the appropriate competencies.

This isn't easy to do. In fact, it can be counterintuitive for salespeople. It requires new behaviors, such "seeking" rather than "telling" and putting *mutual* value first—even if it requires foregoing a deal. But it's essential for successful selling in today's marketplace.

Follow Stapleton's model and the only party who won't win . . . is your competitor.

Rick Justice
Senior Vice President
Worldwide Field Operations
Cisco Systems

Introduction

When I started work on this book, I thought about calling it *Death—and Rebirth—of the Salesman*. I considered the title because *Death of a Salesman* still resonates, especially with those of us who share Willy Loman's vocation.

More than fifty years after Arthur Miller wrote the play, the image of Willy Loman, both self-deluding and self-defeating, still haunts us. It is what our fathers (yes, the field was mostly male then) feared becoming, and it remains the archetype of a person whose life and trade has passed him by. But who is Willy Loman? Some "old guy" past his chronological prime? No. He's a metaphor for anyone paralyzed by fear of change.

Working with thousands of salespeople over the years, I've seen many who are stuck in their ways at a very young age, fearful of any kind of personal change. I've seen equal numbers of "old salts," who are remarkably adaptive to the new realities of their profession. Perhaps that's why they're still in sales—because they have both the clear vision to see when change is necessary and the courage to make that change.

Ultimately, this book isn't about the *death* of the salesman; it's about his *rebirth*. It's not about a tragic past; it's about an exciting future. So let's retire Willy as an image of our insecurities. Let's exorcise the ghost of Willy Loman, just as we need to exorcise the old way of selling. We've entered a new era of business with a new way of selling—the one I've written about in this book. The age of the salesperson as Business Resource, instead of Vendor. Of valued colleague, instead of peddler.

But Willy deserves a retirement tribute, and for that I turn to my friend and associate Dave Matlow who, years ago, coached me through my own transformation from "process engineering" to "process selling." Dave is founder of IMPAX Corporation, a Connecticut-based consulting firm. I'm grateful to Dave for sharing his work and its innovative perspective. Is his tribute disturbing? You bet. Yet I believe it's a useful and sober reminder of our fate as sales professionals, not from growing *old* but from growing *stale*.

It is my hope that this book will, in some way, contribute to whatever personal change *you* are looking to achieve as a member of this profession that I love.

Jerry Stapleton
Elm Grove, Wisconsin

In Memory of Willy
by Dave Matlow

A while ago, I read the Ring Lardner short story "Haircut" about a salesman who, at the turn of the century, was selling canned goods. One day he lost his job. He tried to amuse himself and his friends when he said, "I been sellin' canned goods and [now] I'm canned goods myself."

I'm a salesman. My territory is New England. It's been that way for the past thirty years. I travel to Boston every few months. They like me there. I made friends with the big guy's secretary. I always ask about her kids, who I know by name. The secretary likes me a lot. She gets me past the purchasing agent, ahead of all the other salesmen and then gets me right in to see Mr. Big himself, you know . . . the guy with all the clout.

I make big commissions in Boston. That is, when they buy. Then when I drive home, I smile to myself. I'll soon see the admiration in the eyes of my family when it's time to add up my commissions. They'll be able to make payments on all those nice things that they bought last Christmas.

On Saturdays I wash and shine my car. A guy has got to look successful to his neighbors. We all know that. And my neighbors know that I'm a top salesman in my company. They've been to my house. They have seen the shiny trophies, glossy wall plaques and framed twenty-five-years-of-service award on the wall next to the group picture showing me shaking hands with my boss.

But my son doesn't want to be like me. He doesn't want to follow me in my New England territory. He wants to do something else. He says that he wants to find himself. He doesn't see how important it is for everyone to like him. When he was a small kid, he liked me and wanted to grow up to be like me. We went to Boston together back then.

He saw how I knew everyone's name and their kids' names and how glad they were to see me. But today he's different than when he was a small boy. He says that I don't understand. That hurts me a lot. It makes me long for the past. I wonder if we could just drive to Boston one more time some day. Just another trip to Boston. Together. Just the two of us.

Anyway, I can't forget another time back when I was with the company for about ten years. The Boss surprised me at a company meeting. It was at a branch dinner. He stood up tall, tapped his water glass with a fork and asked them to stop talking and to listen up. Then he told them that I was the top salesman that month. That I was the guy they should all try to copy. That I was the one guy who was always making calls at eight in the morning, who knew which buyers were there to call on.

Sometimes the Boss would help me to be a hero at home, too. He would say it was okay to take my family to dinner and put it on my expense account. He knew that I liked that and how it made my family like the company, too.

That was then. This is now. In recent years my bonuses haven't been as good as they were in the early days. The company has fallen on hard times. The products have become a bit outdated. Competitors are making better products, selling them for lower prices, and hiring more salespeople in my territory. And the customers want to pay only the lowest price, no matter what. Knowing everyone's name isn't worth nearly as much as it used to be.

Younger salespeople who don't know the territory are selling products they don't understand to people they don't know and doing it for companies that they're not loyal to and for more money than they know how to handle.

I just don't have that ginger in my step any longer. It's tough getting up for that early morning call. I fight with my wife over all the unnecessary bills that come in the mail every day. I spend more time reading the papers. Maybe cleaning out the inside of the car and wiping off the hood and headlights with a damp cloth before going to work.

The new boss. He's my old boss's son. I remember the day he was born. His father asked me what to name him. Now, I don't think that the boss's son likes me as much as his father did. I think he wants someone other than me to represent our company in Boston. I should never have yelled at him last year. I was just frustrated. Oh, God, what did I do?

And things have changed in our neighborhood, too. There used to be big trees and plenty of shrubs and flowers around them. Now there's all that litter from the con-struction of all those big, sprawling, so-called starter houses in nearby lots that those Wall Street financial whiz kids are building.

I don't feel as well as I used to. My wife says that it's normal. I don't think it's normal at all. She tells the kids to be respectful of me. What does she mean when she tells them that "attention must be paid"?

I think that something has happened. Something that just isn't right.

I think that my family senses something, too. I think they're a bit uneasy. You see, I'm the breadwinner. I've always been the breadwinner. Everyone counts on me. And my kids. I've always been proud of my kids. But they're old enough now. They've seen how to do it. How I did it. They're my kids. They haven't found their way yet. But they'll do okay. Won't they? I know they will. I'm Willy Loman. I'm their father. And I'm very tired.

Transforming the
Sales Force
for the New Era of Selling

From Vendor
to Business
Resource

"Driving to customer calls, white-shirted and neatly coifed, the salesman seems to have changed little in decades."

—*The Economist*

DEATH OF THE VENDOR

A company from Oshkosh, Wisconsin, whose vehicles had been extremely visible in Operation Desert Storm, found itself one of four manufacturers competing for a large military contract.

As the list eventually narrowed, only one other company posed a challenge to the Oshkosh Truck Company. The final step in the selection process was a face-off between the two competing vehicles. Water, sand, deep mud, steep inclines—the military came up with the most abusive off-road conditions imaginable.

Although the contest had been designed to cover several days, within a few hours both vehicles returned to the starting gate. One of them had gotten stuck in the mud and was being towed by the vehicle from the Oshkosh firm—which, by gosh, won the contract.

That kind of product dominance makes salespeople drool. They get to tell the story over and over to every prospect, winning one deal after another.

But selling no longer works that way. Product superiority, especially the kind of product domination enjoyed by our salivating truck salesperson, has increasingly become the stuff of dreams—and just as elusive. Amid

> PRODUCT SUPERIORITY HAS INCREASINGLY BECOME THE STUFF OF DREAMS—AND JUST AS ELUSIVE.

fevered competition and rapid-fire technological development, innovations last about as long as a Hollywood marriage. No one stays "King of the Hill" for very long.

In the 1980s and '90s, business-to-business companies tried to rise to this challenge by "selling" their way to competitive advantage. "We'll differentiate ourselves through our sales force!" became their collective mantra. So companies ran their salespeople through any number of popular "strategic" sales training programs.

Many of those companies would argue to this day that their approach really made a difference. Perhaps. But if it did, why was turnover among top sales performers so high as they jumped from one hot-product company to the next? It's simple. The game was still all about pitting product Tweedledum against product Tweedledee, with the spoils going largely to the sales reps who were most persuasive in communicating information about their product—and lucky enough to get the best territories.

But that's old news. The nearly complete absence of a *sustainable* competitive advantage through product superiority is yesterday's business story. So is the failed notion that somehow the sales force can compensate by sheer "salesmanship" or by trying to show some value-added goodies that would swing a deal. These realities are the sales rep's first problem.

The second—and infinitely more serious—problem is that the sales rep's customers just don't need him anymore! At least not the way they used to. Distill selling to its essence and you see two things that salespeople have always done to bring value to customers: communicate information and facilitate transactions. Almost overnight these two core functions of the salesperson have lost their value.

"Initially, sales reps were horrified to have pricing, one of their most powerful tools, wrenched from their grasp," said George Roberts, the head of Oracle's North American sales division in the April 22, 2000, issue of *The*

"WE'LL DIFFERENTIATE OURSELVES THROUGH OUR SALES FORCE!" BECAME THEIR COLLECTIVE MANTRA. SO COMPANIES RAN THEIR SALESPEOPLE THROUGH ANY NUMBER OF POPULAR "STRATEGIC" SALES TRAINING PROGRAMS.

THE NEARLY COMPLETE ABSENCE OF A *SUSTAINABLE* COMPETITIVE ADVANTAGE THROUGH PRODUCT SUPERIORITY IS YESTERDAY'S BUSINESS STORY.

Economist. Salespeople would say, "My value-add before was negotiating contracts. What's my value-add now?" These functions, the lifeblood of the selling profession, are diminishing in value as certainly as a new era of selling is replacing the old. Customers won't pay for them and soon won't even tolerate them—and they're making that known to their suppliers.

In a 1998 survey, *Sales & Marketing Management* found that in the two preceding years, the average company's sales force had shrunk by 26 percent—a loss of one position in every four. "And the shrinkage isn't limited to a few industries," the magazine warned. Other studies indicate that half or more of all sales positions will disappear in the coming years.

Incredibly, the technological and economic forces that have rocked every industry and profession in the galaxy over the past few decades have left the selling profession untouched. The April 22, 2000, edition of *The Economist* summed it up this way:

> In all the upheaval that has been brought about by changing technology, one constant has remained. Somehow, where so many denizens of the high-tech world have acquired purple hair and started bringing their budgerigars to work, the sales force has kept its aura of the 1960's Organisation Man. Driving to customer calls, white-shirted and neatly coifed, the salesman seems to have changed little in decades.

Neil Rackham, author of the best-selling *Spin Selling*, used the metaphor of a corporate Rip van Winkle in his 1999 book, coauthored with John DeVincentis, *Rethinking the Sales Force*. Mr. van Winkle wakes after thirty years, not recognizing anything in the corporate landscape. He goes from one department to the next, desperately seeking something familiar.

Only after reaching the sales department does old R.v.W. succeed in his search. Sales looks the same as it did when he fell asleep thirty years earlier.

INCREDIBLY, THE TECHNOLOGICAL AND ECONOMIC FORCES THAT HAVE ROCKED EVERY INDUSTRY AND PROFESSION IN THE GALAXY OVER THE PAST FEW DECADES HAVE LEFT THE SELLING PROFESSION UNTOUCHED.

Selling Isn't About "Selling" Anymore

Selling is no longer a world of overcoming objections, educating customers, negotiating deals, conducting demos, answering technical questions, or any of the other well-known traditional selling activities. Nor is it merely about the terribly misunderstood notion of "relationship building."

The very reason for the existence of salespeople, as we have always understood their purpose, is disappearing.

Words like "good closer," "persuasive," "smooth," "glib," "aggressive," and "personable" have become selling's great anachronisms. The notion of the star salesperson as someone who could sell fleas to a hound dog is gravely out of touch with this new reality.

Way back on July 25, 1994, *Fortune* ran a prophetic piece—particularly so because it was pre-Internet (as we now know it)—titled "The Death and Rebirth of the Salesman." The words of Bill Gardner, 23-year veteran of IBM, now retired, sum up the consummate old-era salesperson:

> I sold systems that people didn't want, didn't need, and couldn't afford. . . . Not so long ago, many salespeople might have regarded [this] admission as the mark of a colleague at the top of his game, one so skilled he could persuade people to act against their own interests. Today, his dubious achievement is more likely to be seen as embarrassing, unenlightened, counterproductive, and even, under some new compensation systems, a shortcut to a smaller bonus.

Or consider the similarly prophetic comments, also back in 1994, from Avrum Lank of the *Milwaukee Sentinel* in his article, "Art of the Sale":

> Why, then, do salespeople get so little respect? Because memorable sales are the painful ones. They occur when a salesperson beats a customer over the head instead of getting inside that head. They occur when a salesperson sells what he has, not what the customer wants.

Sales professionals with years' worth of relationships with their customers are now finding (although they seldom

WORDS LIKE "GOOD CLOSER," "PERSUASIVE," "SMOOTH," "GLIB," "AGGRESSIVE," AND "PERSONABLE" HAVE BECOME SELLING'S GREAT ANACHRONISMS.

admit it) that those relationships aren't buying them the business they used to. Executives and business owners are getting the gnawing feeling that they're paying their salespeople too much—way too much—for what has become a considerably diminished value contribution.

The new sales professional has a new focus: demand creation, philosophical alignment, business fit, positioning, executive credibility, and organizational savvy. These are just a few of the somewhat esoteric-sounding concerns of the new era salesperson. You'll learn about all of them in the coming pages.

Indeed, many of the requirements for a salesperson's success in this new environment are at polar extremes from those that made salespeople successful in the past. One example, which we explore in detail later, is the need to operate in "seek" mode—a notion antithetical to the "tell" mode that has until now been the trademark of the selling profession.

It's (Still) the Web, Stupid!

The dot-com implosion is yesterday's news. For most industries and professions, the so-called "Internet Revolution" has turned out to be anything but. What a surprise—physical factors play a part after all! In many cases, they play the dominant part and affect an industry far more than does the Internet. For example, retailing is more about moving boxes around than it is about the ease of ordering stuff; airlines are more affected by weather and mechanical breakdowns than they are by the effectiveness of their online reservation system; and manufacturing companies live or die more by the quality and cost of their products than by the size of their Web-based supply chain. As a result, the overnight demise of huge industries—so widely predicted—never came to pass.

At the height of dot-com fever, many were also predicting the overnight demise of the salesperson. This didn't come to pass, either. Now, many salespeople not only

INDEED, MANY OF THE REQUIREMENTS FOR A SALESPERSON'S SUCCESS IN THIS NEW ENVIRONMENT ARE AT POLAR EXTREMES FROM THOSE THAT MADE SALESPEOPLE SUCCESSFUL IN THE PAST.

think they dodged that Internet bullet, but they believe it was only a virtual bullet from the get-go.

Not so. Salespeople make a big mistake to conclude that the Internet's threat to them is no more real than it is to the local funeral parlor. As *Business Week* put it in its March 26, 2001, issue:

> Patience, please—the Net obviously won't change everything. Its power to transform will play out unevenly and in stages. . . . Strip away all the highfalutin' talk, and at bottom, the Internet is a tool that dramatically lowers the cost of communication. That means it can radically alter any industry or activity that depends heavily on the flow of information.

Strip away all the highfalutin' talk, and, at bottom, selling is an activity that depends heavily on the flow of information! So while inertia alone will keep selling from an overnight demise, make no mistake about it: We are at the dawn of a new era of selling that will put an end to the need for salespeople *as we've always known them*.

Three aspects of this new era of selling—all tied to the Internet—are causing a fundamental redefinition of the business of selling: (1) computers are free, bandwidth is free; (2) it's an auction economy; and (3) purchasing has truly become strategic.

SO WHILE INERTIA ALONE WILL KEEP SELLING FROM AN OVERNIGHT DEMISE, MAKE NO MISTAKE ABOUT IT: WE ARE AT THE DAWN OF A NEW ERA OF SELLING THAT WILL PUT AN END TO THE NEED FOR SALESPEOPLE *AS WE'VE ALWAYS KNOWN THEM.*

1. **Computers are free, bandwidth is free**. Exaggeration? Only a little! This, in fact, was the premise on which the CEO of a well-known Silicon Valley firm urged me, and a handful of other executives and business owners in a meeting, to build our companies' futures.

   It's not too far off. The price-to-performance ratio of computers today is almost ten thousand times greater than only twenty years ago. And bandwidth? One fiber-optic communications technology called WDM will, according to the December 7, 1998, issue of *Business Week*, "transmit at 200 terabytes per second . . . enough to download the entire Library of Congress every single second. It's mind-boggling." And if that's not fast enough, *The Wall Street Journal* of January 15, 2000, said: "More information can be sent over a single cable in a second today than all the information that was sent over the entire Internet in one month in 1997."

The result? Businesses and consumers have more information at their fingertips than ever before. Remember when Wal-Mart was the innovator with expensive electronic data interchange systems that automatically informed suppliers when their inventories were low at its retail stores around the country? Today such technology is standard throughout retailing. You don't even need complex EDI systems anymore—just do it on the Web. And it's practically free.

Back in 1997, Andy Grove, then CEO of Intel Corp., wrote in an interview with *Sales & Marketing Management* magazine:

> The next strategic inflection point is coming in the form of the Internet, and its greatest impact will hit squarely in your company's sales organization. Everything is going to be touched and reshaped to the very basic principle that the customer and information are as close to each other as the customer and salesperson had been.
>
> The sales structure of the future is going to be different. . . . Salespeople are not going to be involved with order-taking and information flow at the most basic level.

Yet order-taking and information flow represent the lion's share of the traditional salesperson's job. The rest of it—relationship building—is vastly overrated, or at least terribly misunderstood, as *Business Week* reported on March 22, 1999: "So if you're surviving on schmoozy sales relationships, you're not going to make it in this world."

And there will be no letup. It's no longer even news that customers know more about their range of product

ORDER-TAKING AND INFORMATION FLOW REPRESENT THE LION'S SHARE OF THE TRADITIONAL SALESPERSON'S JOB.

**CUSTOMER IGNORANCE
ABOUT PRICING AND
RELATIVE PRODUCT
PERFORMANCE HAD BEEN
A PROFIT CENTER FOR
MANY SUPPLIERS.**

and pricing options than do the suppliers themselves. Customer ignorance about pricing and relative product performance had been a profit center for many suppliers. It's payback time; the balance of power has shifted to the customer.

But don't take my word for it. Ask the salespeople who call on Rite Aid drug stores, the large pharmacy chain. Rite Aid recently announced it would no longer deal with salespeople—its attempt to reduce costs and speed up its buying process.

Ask the Hewlett-Packard vice president of sales who told *The Wall Street Journal* on November 4, 1998: "Leading hospital chains want one-stop shopping on the Internet. With a few mouse clicks, these customers could buy everything from ultrasound machines to electrodes without ever seeing a salesman."

One year later, on December 3, 1999, *The Wall Street Journal* reported: "Within hours of each other last month, GM and Ford rocked Silicon Valley by unveiling plans to set up massive rival online bazaars for all the goods and services they buy—everything from paper clips to stamping presses to contract manufacturing." The reason? "[A]uto makers hope to save billions by replacing an elaborate network of personal contacts with a global electronic forum where deals can be done almost instantly."

2. **It's an auction economy.** The Internet—combined with another long-standing megatrend, the commoditization of almost everything—makes for another lesser, yet still significant, factor transforming selling: the auction economy.

   "Going, Going, Gone! The B2B Tool That Really Is Changing the World," read the *Fortune* headline of March 20, 2000. The article went on to tell how Web auctions are revolutionizing the $5 trillion market for industrial parts. "No more golf-course schmoozing," the article said, "no more haggling, no more sealed bids."

The article continued, "This FreeMarkets auction idea is revolutionizing procurement as we know it," said Kent Britten, vice president of supply management for United Technologies, a global manufacturing and technology company.

In a story two months later on Web auctions, *Fortune*, on May 1, 2000, added: "This is a genuine revolution. It ought to terrify everyone who sells anything to businesses. . . . And it's just getting started."

As much as two years earlier, on December 7, 1998, *Fortune* had reported: "Customers are about to get much, much better informed—and the consequences will be awe-inspiring. . . . So if your product is anything close to a commodity, prices will trend downward toward variable costs, and margins will be skinnier than an anorexic supermodel."

Because many of the online marketplaces have met with a similar fate as other dot-coms, some salespeople feel that electronic business-to-business commerce is yet another virtual bullet. Sure, a few fatal flaws handicapped the earliest online marketplace business models, not the least of which was making far too much sensitive information available to competitors. But the economics of B-to-B commerce are way too attractive to dismiss. So companies have simply tweaked the business model to change from public to private exchanges.

The Wall Street Journal weighed in on this issue on March 16, 2001, in a piece titled "'Private Exchanges' May Allow B-to-B Commerce to Thrive After All." Conclusion: "B-to-B commerce isn't dead. Instead, a growing number of companies are turning to 'private exchanges' to link with a specially invited group of suppliers and partners over the Web." Yes, indeed, the consequences will still inspire awe in salespeople—at least to those with their eyes open.

> "THIS IS A GENUINE REVOLUTION. IT OUGHT TO TERRIFY EVERYONE WHO SELLS ANYTHING TO BUSINESSES. . . . AND IT'S JUST GETTING STARTED."
> —*FORTUNE*

3. Purchasing has truly become strategic. Not long ago, the notion of "strategic purchasing" would have been an oxymoron. An assignment to the Purchasing Department was the corporate kiss of death for one's career. Purchasing is where one went to "beat up on vendors." Indeed, this remains the case at many companies. But it's changing.

Companies have found it too expensive to continue embracing the old practice of shopping many vendors to compare unit prices in search of the mythical "best deal." They realize that doing so brings with it other, intrinsic costs that can make this form of bargain-hunting a penny-wise, dollar-foolish proposition.

One study, reported in the 1997 annual report of the office supplier Corporate Express Corporation, found that "each time a company purchases $100 worth of nonproduction supplies, it spends an additional $150 to cover the cost of ordering, processing, and delivering those goods. Obviously, purchasing is an expensive process for large corporations around the world."

Fewer, more integral supplier relationships are one result of this trend. Not long ago I conducted a joint call with a client of mine at a Fortune 100 manufacturing company. During our visit, we learned that the company was in the throes of a major vendor reduction program, cutting its vendor count from 55,000 to 1,750, more than a 90 percent reduction. Few corporations have not undergone similar supplier reductions.

What we've come to know as "purchasing" is being changed forever by sophisticated supply-chain models that incorporate such concepts as total cost of ownership, strategic significance to the buying company's business, and the availability of substitutes.

What's more, the RFQ (Request for Quotation) process has died and been reborn—a development tightly related to the auction economy. The bane of selling companies, RFQs have a longstanding tradition of sapping resources—that "giant sucking sound" you hear—most often resulting in an unfavorable decision, with the spoils going to the bidder who did the best job of prewiring the deal.

Many salespeople thought that the RFQ process would, in one of the few positive outcomes of the new era of selling, disappear. Guess again. Said Free-Markets' CEO Glen Meakem in a March 20, 2000, *Fortune* interview, "The problem [with the traditional RFQ process] lies in the hidebound and opaque RFQ tradition."

The interviewer noted, "To unshackle the power of the purchaser, his [Meakem's] system turns the once secretive RFQ into an open bidding war. It does that by standardizing absolutely everything in the RFQ. That way each package is practically the same; plastic refrigerator shelves and automobile bumpers become almost as much a commodity as bushels of wheat."

Add to these three forces today's skyrocketing cost of a face-to-face sales call ($600, according to the latest estimate), and you have the impetus for massive change. Companies can ill afford to put feet on the street for anything but the highest-impact activities involving the best-qualified, most-profitable opportunities. Yet it's amazing how much they ignore this reality, deriving some vague, fuzzy comfort from merely—and often aimlessly—putting themselves in front of the customer.

The megatrends we're seeing are combining to spell the eventual, but certain, demise of the *traditional* salesperson—the Vendor.

Sales today has an entirely new business model and demands an entirely new type of sales professional. Some companies will decide they don't need sales reps at all. One East Coast technology company not long ago converted its entire business to alternate channels, completely eliminating a stunned field sales force of two hundred.

SALES TODAY HAS AN ENTIRELY NEW BUSINESS MODEL AND DEMANDS AN ENTIRELY NEW TYPE OF SALES PROFESSIONAL.

The cover story of the March 2000 issue of *Sales & Marketing Management* was titled, "Is Your Job in Jeopardy? Don't Be a Victim of the New Economy. Here's How to Survive."

The primary mission of sales professionals who embrace this new paradigm is to create demand for their companies and create value for their customers. "Intel reps don't sell products. They create demand," said Andy Grove.

As the old business model for selling becomes permanently obsolete and the "salesman" fades into the sunset, a new business model is emerging. Quoting Rackham and DeVincentis again:

> Irresistible new forces are reshaping the world of selling. Sales functions everywhere are in the early stages of radical and profound changes comparable to those that began in manufacturing 20 years ago. . . . But one change outweighs all the others. The meaning of selling itself is shifting. The very purpose of sales is being rapidly redefined.

Or consider the comment from Thomas Siebel and Pat House in their book, *Cyber Rules*. "What we mean by 'sales' is undergoing a radical redefinition."

But merely recognizing the existence of this new business model for selling is the easy part. As they say, "It's in all the papers." For salespeople, knowing how to implement that model is the hard part. That's what this book is about.

THE PRIMARY MISSION OF SALES PROFESSIONALS WHO EMBRACE THIS NEW PARADIGM IS TO CREATE DEMAND FOR THEIR COMPANIES AND CREATE VALUE FOR THEIR CUSTOMERS.

chapter 2

"The sales structure of the future is going to be different. Salespeople are not going to be involved with order-taking and information flow at the most basic level."

—Andy Grove, Co-founder, Intel Corporation

March 1997

BIRTH OF THE BUSINESS RESOURCE

"Selling" has a whole new definition. In fact, selling requires more than simply a change in the meaning of the term—it requires a whole new term. In the same way, "salesperson" needs a whole new definition.

The term I use to define the old-paradigm salesperson is Vendor/Problem-Solver. I call the new breed of salesperson the Business Resource.

Are you a Vendor/Problem-Solver on the endangered species list? If so, are you ready to undergo the DNA-level change to Business Resource with a bright, professionally rewarding future? Here's what it takes.

Start by acknowledging that customers are perceiving your value based more on *how* you sell than on *what* you sell. They see you for what you are and the value *you* bring, not for the product you carry or the company you represent.

Here's what happened to someone who sells paper to large printing companies. After he recently closed a big deal, his customer called his company and asked if the salesperson had received a commission on the sale.

"Yes," came the paper company's response.

"How much?"

"Five percent."

"Good," said the customer. "Then I want my invoice reduced by five percent, because he brought no value to the sale."

By contrast, an acquaintance of mine who represents a large chemical company was invited by the president of one of his customer firms to sit on the customer's strategic planning team to help the company develop long-term strategies. This acquaintance sells printing supplies, films, and chemicals—products that many view as commodities.

Who's the Vendor/Problem-Solver and who's the Business Resource? To the uninitiated, the two may look the same and appear to do similar things in their sales approaches. But there are differences—sometimes subtle on their surface but profound in their impact.

Fig. 2-1

THE CUSTOMER'S PERCEPTION OF YOUR VALUE

I USE A DOTTED LINE BETWEEN VENDOR AND PROBLEM-SOLVER TO REPRESENT THE SMALL DIFFERENCE THAT EXISTS BETWEEN THE TWO.

What are those differences? Figure 2-1 illustrates the three levels at which customers perceive a salesperson's value. I use a dotted line between Vendor and Problem-Solver to represent the small difference that exists between the two. In fact, it's because that difference is so slight that I combine them as the Vendor/Problem-Solver. I use a double solid line between Problem-Solver and Business Resource to symbolize the twofold barrier that exists to becoming a Business Resource. One of these barriers is the *personal* change that a salesperson must undergo to transform him or herself. The other is the cultural and procedural barriers within the *selling company itself* that can hinder—or prevent—the transformation. I explain those cultural and procedural barriers more in Chapter 10.

Where on this pyramid are you? Here's a quick assessment to help you find out.

DO YOU STILL LOOK FOR THE "DECISION-MAKER," OR ARE YOU ORGANIZATIONALLY SAVVY?

If you're a Vendor/Problem-Solver . . .
Your motto is "look for the decision-maker"; you overlook the complexity of decision-making processes in customer organizations, where crucial purchasing decisions turn on the ebb and flow of shifting influence. You assume someone with a big title is automatically someone with big power. You ignore, are a victim of, or are oblivious to political forces, which always trump business reasons for a buying decision.

If you're a Business Resource . . .
You consider "decision-maker" a meaningless term. You recognize that organizational dynamics in the real world are complex and subtle. You understand that title and influence don't always go together, and you make it your business to figure out who in the customer firm may have high influence despite having a low title—and vice versa. You know that your sales plan is only as strong as the contacts that support it, and that contacts with the most influence are the hardest ones for you to reach. You never ask a contact: "Who makes the decision?" or "Who else should I be talking to?"

You also recognize that customers place great value on your ability to make things happen for their benefit in your own company. Knowing this, you make certain that you demonstrate organizational savvy to your customers so that they place their trust—and the value that goes with it—in you to act effectively as their advocate in your company.

Do You Gravitate to "Comfortable Contacts," or Are You Executive Credible?

If you're a Vendor/Problem-Solver . . .

You dismiss the importance of getting to senior executives. You think, "I'll alienate my contact" . . . "The decision just goes to senior management for a rubber stamp" . . . "The real decision-makers are the worker bees here" . . . or "Executives don't get involved in what we sell." If you're a techie type, you like to call on techie types. If you do find yourself in front of an executive, you treat the meeting like your meetings with lower-level folks, discussing your company and solution or conducting a needs analysis or demo.

If you're a Business Resource . . .

You're executive credible. It's your standard operating procedure to approach senior management. You know when and how to do it, and you understand what it takes to be viewed by the company's executives as a Business Resource, not a Vendor, and thus get invited back. What's more, you're able to do this not only without alienating lower-level contacts, but often with their encouragement because they see you as someone who can bring them valuable visibility with the boss.

If you're a Business Resource . . . You're executive credible. It's your standard operating procedure to approach senior management.

Do You Rely More on Proposals or on Business Presentations?

If you're a Vendor/Problem-Solver . . .

Your principal sales tool is the proposal, ignoring the fact that most are about as inspirational as a consumer brochure on aluminum siding. If you lose a sale, you have a ready excuse: "What can I say, boss? They just didn't like our proposal."

A Business Presentation (and you'll learn more about the Business Presentation in Chapter 7) to an executive, without your product in the middle to protect you, is probably more than your comfort zone can handle.

If you're a Business Resource . . .
Your principal sales tool is the Business Presentation. You know that nothing has a higher impact in the sales cycle, and that an effective stand-up presentation is much more compelling than sitting across a table discussing your solution, proposal, or company. You view the proposal as a confirmation tool, not a sales tool.

IF YOU'RE A BUSINESS RESOURCE . . .
YOU VIEW THE PROPOSAL AS A CONFIRMATION TOOL, NOT A SALES TOOL.

DO YOU QUALIFY BY GUT FEEL, OR DO YOU ASSESS OPPORTUNITIES WITH OBJECTIVE CRITERIA?

If you're a Vendor/Problem-Solver . . .
You rely on your gut feelings and hunches to qualify opportunities. As a result, you spend too much time pursuing sales opportunities that you end up losing ("I'm no quitter!") and too much time on opportunities that, with far less effort and fewer company resources, you'd succeed in getting anyway ("They love me in Omaha!"). You reason that a big account is automatically a good account. You hate bad news and go to great lengths to avoid it.

If you're a Business Resource . . .
You force every sales opportunity to pass a three-part test: (1) Should we pursue this? (2) Can we win? (3) Will it be good business? You use objective criteria for answering these questions, and you're diligent about using them because you know that assessing the kind of relationship the two companies can and should have is one of the highest value activities you can undertake. You recognize that a prospect company's value orientation—that is, how it assigns value to your product or service, not its size—is what determines how "good" a customer that prospect is likely to be. You hate bad news, too, but if you're going to get it, you want it early.

IF YOU'RE A BUSINESS RESOURCE . . .
YOU FORCE EVERY SALES OPPORTUNITY TO PASS A THREE-PART TEST: (1) SHOULD WE PURSUE THIS? (2) CAN WE WIN? (3) WILL IT BE GOOD BUSINESS?

ARE YOU SATISFIED WITH SALES ACTIVITY, OR DO YOU AIM TO OWN THE CUSTOMER?

If you're a Vendor/Problem-Solver . . .
Your purpose in life is sales activity. You rack up stacks of proposals, fire off quotes, do the demos, answer customers' technical questions, wear your index finger out making phone calls, and figure it will all help you make the customer's short list or even close the sale. Nobody can say you don't work hard.

IF YOU'RE A BUSINESS RESOURCE . . . YOUR GOAL ISN'T TO GENERATE ACTIVITY BUT TO "OWN" THE CUSTOMER.

If you're a Business Resource . . .
Your goal isn't to generate activity but to "own" the customer. Your goal is to reach a relationship in which customers turn to you first whenever they have a need that you can be reasonably expected to fill. You strive to be seen as having much broader value than that of a mere vendor. You constantly assess your own selling activities, calibrating them against known standards for "high-impact activities."

DO YOU FULFILL OPPORTUNITIES, OR DO YOU CREATE THEM?

If you're a Vendor/Problem-Solver . . .
You're content with fulfilling known opportunities with known solutions. "Is there a budget?" you ask, then try to show the customer that your solution is the best one within that constraint. You learn about your own product line so you can offer it as the answer to your customers' problems.

IF YOU'RE A BUSINESS RESOURCE . . . YOU KNOW THAT WHEN A COMPANY WANTS TO DO SOMETHING, IT WILL FIND THE BUDGET DOLLARS AND NOT BE LIMITED BY EXISTING BUDGETS.

If you're a Business Resource . . .
You create opportunities—and value. You understand that if you know the customer's business well enough, you may see a need before the customer does. You know that when a company wants to do something, it will find the budget dollars and not be limited by existing budgets. You take responsibility for possessing superlative product knowledge, knowing that it's the minimum ante just to be in the game. But you focus most of your energy on acquiring a deep

knowledge of your customer's business and on gaining access to the executive levels where budgets are blessed and the value you create is recognized.

DO YOU RELY ON PRICE, PRODUCT, AND PERSISTENCE, OR DO YOU RELY ON STRATEGY?

If you're a Vendor/Problem-Solver . . .

You like nothing more than a good competitive fight. You'll outsell competitors on whatever grounds they choose—price, product specifications, quality—who cares? You're also supremely confident that you can win almost any battle by force of your personality or your responsiveness. You're a relationship builder and put a lot of stock in these relationships. Of course, you call just about everything you do a "strategy."

If you're a Business Resource . . .

You know the real contest isn't about price, specifications, or quality. It's about value, strategy, and positioning. You not only take responsibility to position yourself and win the sale, you also take responsibility to position your competitors and make sure they lose the sale. Unlike the Vendor/Problem-Solver, you understand the profound difference between "strategy" and "tactic."

IF YOU'RE A BUSINESS RESOURCE . . . YOU ALSO TAKE RESPONSIBILITY TO POSITION YOUR COMPETITORS AND MAKE SURE THEY LOSE THE SALE.

DO YOU OPERATE IN "TELL" MODE OR "SEEK" MODE?

If you're a Vendor/Problem-Solver . . .

Because you see your reason for existence as communicating information, you operate in "tell" mode. You do listen, of course, but it's an aimless, perfunctory listening in which you seek only signs of a need for your product. At best, your conversations with customers are the traditional find-the-need/describe-the-solution dialogue. At worst, you see selling as a game of trying to say the thing about your solution that hits the customer's hot button. The way you work resembles the line: "Stop me when you hear something you like." You are the caricature of a Vendor.

IF YOU'RE A BUSINESS
RESOURCE . . .
YOU LISTEN BEYOND THE
NEED. YOUR QUESTIONS
AREN'T THE MYOPIC,
FIND-THE-NEED
QUESTIONS OF THE
VENDOR/PROBLEM-
SOLVER.

If you're a Business Resource . . .

You operate in "seek" mode. You know that the only way you can create demand for your company and value for the customer is to listen with a very disciplined and strategic sense of curiosity. You listen beyond the need. Your questions aren't the myopic, find-the-need questions of the Vendor/Problem-Solver. Your questions seek to give you a holistic view of the customer's company.

You apply business judgment and organizational savvy to what you hear. When necessary, you're able to truly leave your solutions at the door, even when the customer seems open to hearing about them or expresses an interest. You know when to deflect such interest—and when not to. You're never afraid of missing an opportunity because you listened too much, potentially failing to tell the customer something that might have prompted him or her to buy.

Do You Attempt to Build Personal Relationships or Business Relationships?

If you're a Vendor/Problem-Solver . . .

You see the customer as your friend and focus on building rapport as your way of achieving success. Or, you might have a feeling of inferiority, using language to send a message to the customer of "Sorry to bother you" or "Thank you for taking time out of your busy schedule to meet with me." This is one reason you are less comfortable meeting with executives.

IF YOU'RE A BUSINESS
RESOURCE . . .
YOU SEE THE CUSTOMER
AS A BUSINESS PEER
BECAUSE YOU HAVE THE
CONFIDENCE THAT YOU
CAN BRING BUSINESS
VALUE TO HIM OR HER.

If you're a Business Resource . . .

You see the customer as a business peer because you have the confidence that you can bring business value to him or her. You express gratitude to customers in a way that conveys both professional courtesy while also conveying confidence that the discussion between you and the customer is a mutually beneficial one. For this same reason, you're even comfortable viewing a customer executive as a business peer.

DO YOU RELY ON EXCEPTIONAL PRODUCT KNOWLEDGE OR EXCEPTIONAL KNOWLEDGE OF THE CUSTOMER'S BUSINESS?

If you're a Vendor/Problem-Solver . . .

You understand the customer's business—but only up to the point that it applies to what you're selling. Your efforts to understand the customer's problems are primarily a search for opportunities to sell your product. Thus, if you're going to be successful, you figure that you'd better have exceptional product knowledge. To you, the pinnacle of selling is conducting a "killer demo." You don't want to admit it, but you're operating according to the principle, "When all you sell is hammers, everything starts looking like a nail."

If you're a Business Resource . . .

You possess superlative product knowledge and can demo with the best of them. You also know when to deploy that knowledge and when to demo. But your real passion is with the customer's business. As you learn it, you are able to temporarily ignore what you're attempting to sell. You view the customer's business through the same lens as that customer's CEO might, not through the lens of a salesperson looking for a "business need" for his or her product. As a result, you've developed the ability to align the value your company brings with the business drivers and initiatives of the customer company. Where the Vendor/Problem-Solver shows only the "solution fit," you show also the "business fit."

IF YOU'RE A BUSINESS RESOURCE . . . YOU VIEW THE CUSTOMER'S BUSINESS THROUGH THE SAME LENS AS THAT CUSTOMER'S CEO MIGHT, NOT THROUGH THE LENS OF A SALESPERSON LOOKING FOR A "BUSINESS NEED" FOR HIS OR HER PRODUCT.

DO YOU ASK THE CUSTOMER FOR THE NEXT STEP, OR DO YOU STEER THE SALES CAMPAIGN YOURSELF?

If you're a Vendor/Problem-Solver . . .

You ask the customer for the next step in a sales campaign. Perhaps that's because you see your role more as service than selling, operating from a "customer-is-always-right" mindset. Maybe you're just more comfortable taking direction from the customer. Or, since you're not really following any sales process, you may not know what the next step should be.

If you're a Business Resource . . .

You steer the sales campaign, and customers are comfortable having you do so because you convey the confidence that you know your craft. You sell using a proven sales process, so you know what the next step should be. You suggest next steps to customers. You seldom ask the customer, "What would you like to do next?"—but you do know when such a question is called for.

IF YOU'RE A BUSINESS RESOURCE . . .
YOU SELL USING A PROVEN SALES PROCESS, SO YOU KNOW WHAT THE NEXT STEP SHOULD BE.

WHEN YOU LOSE A SALE DO YOU SAY "THEY DIDN'T LIKE OUR PRICE OR PRODUCT," OR DO YOU SAY "I WAS OUTSOLD"?

If you're a Vendor/Problem-Solver . . .

You see your role as a conduit of information about your company and its solutions. As a result, when you come in second in a sales campaign, it's natural for you to disengage from the responsibility for defeat. You might say, "Our price was too high" or "We didn't have the features they were looking for" or "It was political," and so on. You may even call the customer in a postmortem so that you can report back what the customer specifically didn't like about your company's offering. Funny, though, when you win a sale, you seem a bit more prepared to accept the credit for great selling.

If you're a Business Resource . . .

You take total responsibility for the process of acquiring the customer, managing the relationship, making the competition lose, qualifying opportunities (as an ongoing process, thus knowing when it might be time to walk), and being aware of the political factors influencing decisions. Therefore, when you lose a sale, you say, "I was outsold," because you failed to manage perfectly some aspect of the sales process. When you win a deal, you're probably more likely to downplay your own role in the victory and credit others from your company who were instrumental in the successful sale.

IF YOU'RE A BUSINESS RESOURCE . . .
WHEN YOU LOSE A SALE, YOU SAY, "I WAS OUTSOLD."

SAY GOOD-BYE TO YOUR COMFORT ZONE

The direct sales force will not merely survive, it will play a critical role in the new era of selling. But it must remake itself to focus on only the highest value, Business Resource–driven activities. It must shed its old, low-value, Vendor/Problem-Solver activities to alternate channels. That's easier said than done because, based on my experience, less than one-fourth of direct salespeople's time is currently spent on true high-value activities.

What's more, this transformation requires salespeople to make some deeply personal decisions about who they are as sales professionals—decisions that will push their comfort zones to the limit. This could be difficult, because salespeople are way, way above average in their aversion to change. But don't ever sell them short, because salespeople are also way above average in their ability to act when their backs are against the wall—and their backs are now against the mother of all walls.

> SALESPEOPLE ARE ALSO WAY ABOVE AVERAGE IN THEIR ABILITY TO ACT WHEN THEIR BACKS ARE AGAINST THE WALL— AND THEIR BACKS ARE NOW AGAINST THE MOTHER OF ALL WALLS.

SAY HELLO TO THE ADVENTURE

If you've read this far, chances are you've accepted my premise that as a sales professional, you need to transform yourself if you want to be a player in the new era of selling. You've probably also accepted the description of the Business Resource as the vision of your transformed self. If so, read on. The rest of this book describes the adventure: the mindset you need to develop, the process you have to embrace, and the skills you must master if you are to breathe life into that vision.

This book is not so much about how to restructure your company or your sales organization to thrive in the new era of selling. It's more about what you—the business-to-business salesperson—should be doing, day by day, to thrive. It's about the high-impact activities that make up the new business of selling.

In the next chapter, I start right out with a tactical discussion on how to implement the most fundamental aspect of selling at the Business Resource level: operating in "seek" mode. In Chapter 4, you learn how to navigate organizations in order to identify who the real power players are. Chapter 5 shows you why and how your customer business knowledge is your most powerful competitive weapon.

In Chapter 6, you discover that something you should be doing in the old paradigm of selling—getting to executives—isn't going away in the new. More important, you learn the two most effective, business-oriented, non-gimmicky approaches for doing so. Chapter 7 talks about why the Business Presentation is the key tactic for successful selling in the new era of selling, and it gives you the step-by-step process for developing it and delivering it.

In Chapter 8, I attempt to condense a few millennia's worth of knowledge and experience about military strategy and other forms of competitive engagement into a few pages called "Pragmatic Positioning." Chapter 9 describes what I believe is the single most important task of the new era salesperson: assessing sales situations to determine what kind of business relationship, if any, the selling and buying company should have in order to yield the highest degree of mutual value.

In the final chapter, I lay out what it will take for you as a sales professional to transform yourself from Vendor/Problem-Solver to Business Resource. I also prescribe the medicine—some bitter—that senior executives must take to support that transformation.

One final note. You might be surprised at some of the competencies I don't include in my discussion of the new era salesperson, such as keeping up with the Internet and other technologies, learning how to deal with cross-channel convergence, or cultivating extraordinary knowledge of your products.

Are these not important? Of course they are. It's just that they're the easy part: it's easy to become Web savvy; it's hard to become organizationally savvy. It's easy to learn to deal with channels; it's hard to learn to deal with executives. It's easy to describe a product fit; it's hard to describe a business fit.

I'm giving you the hard part: the skills which, when properly implemented, will lead you to the essential competencies for success as a new era salesperson.

I'M GIVING YOU THE HARD PART: THE SKILLS WHICH, WHEN PROPERLY IMPLEMENTED, WILL LEAD YOU TO THE ESSENTIAL COMPETENCIES FOR SUCCESS AS A NEW ERA SALESPERSON.

chapter 3

"We are not fit to lead an army unless we are familiar with the face of the country."

—Sun Tzu, *The Art of War*

HOW TO OPERATE IN SEEK MODE

While on a consulting engagement at IBM's Toronto office a few years back, I was waved into the office of the company's head of Canadian sales operations.

"Jerry, what do you think is the one most important characteristic a salesperson must have to be effective?" he asked me.

I could tell from his manner that he'd been pondering the subject for some time and had discovered the answer. Never having given that specific question much thought, I did what any self-respecting consultant would do: I launched into a lengthy response pointing out that it was a combination of things, blah, blah, blah!

Then, also in true-to-form consultant fashion, I asked *his* opinion. His answer was clear, concise, and simple: "A sense of curiosity!"

It hit me immediately that he was right. Sure, there are lots of other very important qualities, such as self-motivation, ego, empathy, and the like, but they're largely rendered inert without a strong sense of curiosity. Indeed, as I thought further about the best salespeople I'd ever worked with, I realized they all had that one characteristic in common—a

> AS I THOUGHT FURTHER ABOUT THE BEST SALESPEOPLE I'D EVER WORKED WITH, I REALIZED THEY ALL HAD THAT ONE CHARACTERISTIC IN COMMON—A SENSE OF CURIOSITY.

sense of curiosity. Strange, isn't it, that when we conjure up the caricature of the "typical" salesperson, just the opposite jumps out at us—the gift of gab?

Perhaps you think this is going to be yet another speech from yet another "sales expert" telling you to listen more. It's not. I've been on countless calls with sales professionals who spent an hour or more simply listening to a customer. Too often it ended up as just that: aimless listening to the customer's relatively aimless talking.

I've also worked with sales pros who can drill down on listening to "customer needs" to the minutest level, returning from the call with pages of notes representing the most thorough needs assessment you'd ever want to see. Then, after losing the deal, they wondered what went wrong, since they knew they'd understood the customer's needs and met them better than the competition.

When I had my epiphany-type encounter with the Canadian IBM executive, selling was still immersed in its old paradigm, and I was not yet aware that selling was in the early stages of being totally redefined. Yet even then, in the older world of traditional selling, a sense of curiosity was a trademark of the select few who could be labeled "great" salespeople. After all, salespeople could still do pretty well if they were particularly skilled at telling customers about their stuff.

> WITH THE VALUE OF "TELL" MODE SELLING EVAPORATING ALMOST OVERNIGHT, A SENSE OF CURIOSITY, PROPERLY HARNESSED, IS PART OF THE "MINIMUM SYSTEM REQUIREMENTS" JUST TO BE IN THE NEW GAME.

In today's new era of selling, however, with the value of "tell" mode selling evaporating almost overnight, a sense of curiosity, properly harnessed, is part of the "minimum system requirements" just to be in the new game.

In Chapter 2, I identify "operating in seek mode" as a trademark of the Business Resource. This chapter is all about developing a seek mode mindset and putting it into practice, mostly in the form of what I simply refer to as Knowledge Calls.

And it does start with the mindset. I can give you all the great sound bites and techniques. But without the right mindset, they are hollow manipulations and will be quickly exposed by customers.

Here's what the right mindset did for Cory, a top sales-person for one of my firm's clients. I had just accompanied Cory on a call to one of his best accounts, one of his company's customers for years. The visit with Cory's midlevel contact, John, had been scheduled for forty-five minutes. But it lasted more than two hours, and it was the customer who wouldn't end the meeting. As we parted, John actually embraced Cory—the first time I ever saw *that* happen. "This was the best meeting our two companies have ever had," John said.

Had Cory mesmerized the customer with a pitch for some hot new product? Just the opposite. We never once talked about products. We were operating completely in seek mode, conducting a true Knowledge Call. Later, Cory explained to me how the visit had differed from his previous information-gathering calls: "When John started talking about some of the challenges he was facing, I naturally wanted to tell him how we could help. But you wouldn't let me."

OPERATING IN SEEK MODE GOES FAR BEYOND MERE INFORMATION-GATHERING

Precisely. Cory's observation summarizes why virtually all salespeople say they operate in seek mode when few really do. Most ask only enough questions to size up the problem their solution will solve, and they quickly abandon the effort if the customer starts asking questions about their wares.

But a true Knowledge Call helps the salesperson build a strategic base of knowledge about the customer. That's why Knowledge Calls are infinitely more powerful than traditional forms of information-gathering calls.

The Knowledge Call is not a needs analysis meeting. Although the salesperson does gain information on customer needs, that isn't the main purpose. Its aim is to gain insight into the customer's organization, its business, its culture, its political structure, and the "fit" between the two companies.

> VIRTUALLY ALL SALESPEOPLE SAY THEY OPERATE IN SEEK MODE WHEN FEW REALLY DO. MOST ASK ONLY ENOUGH QUESTIONS TO SIZE UP THE PROBLEM THEIR SOLUTION WILL SOLVE.

When you conduct a Knowledge Call, you must leave discussions of solutions for another time. This rule is easy on paper, hard in practice. Nevertheless, exercising this discipline not only advances your sale in the long run but repositions you in the customer's mind, elevating you from a mere Vendor or Problem-Solver to a Business Resource.

At this point you may be tempted to breeze right past the rest of this chapter, saying to yourself, "I already do this stuff. We just call it something else in our company"—a discovery call, a needs assessment, fact-finding, or whatever.

WHATEVER YOU CALL IT, IN THE VAST MAJORITY OF ORGANIZATIONS, SUCH CALLS ARE ALMOST ALWAYS CARRIED OUT AS VENDOR/PROBLEM-SOLVER ACTIVITIES, WHICH, AT BEST, SEEK TO FIND ONLY THE ISSUES THAT DRIVE THE NEED FOR THE SALESPERSON'S SOLUTION.

Whatever you call it, in the vast majority of organizations, such calls are almost always carried out as Vendor/Problem-Solver activities, which, at best, seek to find only the issues that drive the need for the salesperson's solution and a few tidbits about the so-called "key decision-makers." The Knowledge Call is the exclusive domain of the Business Resource. All other fact-finding calls are the domain of the Vendor/Problem-Solver.

My firm's consultants routinely conduct joint Knowledge Calls together with my clients' salespeople. Whenever we do, we carry the business cards of our client companies, working as ad hoc members of the client's management team. I've conducted over a thousand of these calls myself. Yet my fingers and toes are more than enough to count the number of salespeople who actually did Knowledge Calls before my firm's involvement.

What often happens is illustrated by the reaction of Sherry, the top strategic accounts salesperson for one of my client companies. During the course of our joint Knowledge Call, which had been textbook up to that point, the customer contact made a passing comment about a purchase they were going to be considering at some time down the road.

Without missing a beat Sherry leaned forward, slapped her hand on the customer's desk, and said, "Can we bid on that?" She caught herself immediately and her eyes shifted to me with a slightly sheepish look that all but admitted, "There it is, that cultural thing." Despite, or more likely as a result of, that experience, Sherry has since become a model Business Resource. Others have had similar experiences.

Knowledge Calls that fall short have two things in common:

1. The salesperson lacks, or fails to exercise, the critically important sense of curiosity, and

2. The salesperson pursues selling opportunities and buying signals that come up in the call.

Another hurdle in keeping a sales representative's attention on the real goal of a Knowledge Call is the high degree of detail, subtlety, and nuance associated with doing a true Knowledge Call. Let's face it: sales reps are not generally known as detail people. Yet it's the little things that determine the difference between a Knowledge Call and a generic information-gathering call.

Clearly, the Knowledge Call isn't a new concept. It's just a much more in-depth version of a concept with which salespeople are already familiar.

My purpose in this chapter is not to convince you of the need to learn more about your customers, their business, their organizations, and the like. Instead, this is a highly tactical chapter, focusing mostly on the "how-to" of Knowledge Calls, addressing such topics as their logistics, how you request them, with whom to conduct them, and how to frame your questions. In fact, in this chapter I don't even address the issue of what to look for in Knowledge Calls. That's covered principally in Chapter 4, "How Organizations *Really* Work," Chapter 5, "Understanding the Customer's Business," and Chapter 9, "Opportunity Assessment."

> THE KNOWLEDGE CALL ISN'T A NEW CONCEPT. IT'S JUST A MUCH MORE IN-DEPTH VERSION OF A CONCEPT WITH WHICH SALESPEOPLE ARE ALREADY FAMILIAR.

HOW A KNOWLEDGE CALL IS DIFFERENT

A Knowledge Call is distinct from other types of sales calls in four primary ways:

1. **Products are truly left at the door.** The aim of a Knowledge Call is not to discuss your company and its solutions. This requires a level of discipline much more difficult than it appears, as Sherry learned when she had a knee-jerk reaction to a future purchasing opportunity.

2. **A Knowledge Call is not only about the buying company's needs.** Customer needs spring from customer business issues. Certainly some discussion of customer needs occurs during a Knowledge Call. The Vendor/Problem-Solver stops there—or, at best, tries to understand the business issues relating to the needs that the salesperson knows he or she can fill. But the Business Resource does much more. The Business Resource seeks to understand not only the business issues behind the customer's immediate needs but also the much broader business issues facing the customer.

3. **A Knowledge Call is positioned with a very specific purpose in mind.** A Business Resource has developed the ability to clearly frame his or her request for a Knowledge Call with directness and clarity. The positioning isn't buried in some fuzzy, general request to "get together" with that customer or to "understand the customer's needs." While this distinction may seem insignificant, it's anything but. How a Knowledge Call is positioned is among the biggest predictors of its success. What's more, whether a Knowledge Call is conducted as a distinct, stand-alone meeting or integrated into another type of sales call, which is common, it must be clearly positioned.

4. **A Knowledge Call doesn't have to yield a lot of knowledge to be useful.** Surprised? Such calls always yield knowledge. But they don't have to. The salesperson succeeds in scoring Business Resource points just for asking good questions. Remember, it's not merely about information gathering; it's also about how you are perceived by your customers.

THE BUSINESS RESOURCE SEEKS TO UNDERSTAND NOT ONLY THE BUSINESS ISSUES BEHIND THE CUSTOMER'S IMMEDIATE NEEDS BUT ALSO THE MUCH BROADER BUSINESS ISSUES FACING THE CUSTOMER.

To view the differences another way, consider the Knowledge Call in relation to some of the elements of a total sales strategy (more on this later).

- How credibly could you articulate knowledge of this customer company's business to its CEO and, in turn, articulate the business fit between your two companies?

- What facts do you have to confirm your perceptions of the real level of influence that your contacts possess? Do you understand the key political agendas?

- Do you know enough about your competition's strategy to launch an effective counterstrategy?

- Can you adequately answer three questions based on objective criteria:

    (1) Should we pursue?

    (2) Can we win?

    (3) Will it be good business?

From the foregoing, it should be clear that only by conducting Knowledge Calls will you be able to develop a strategy for the sale.

> ONLY BY CONDUCTING KNOWLEDGE CALLS WILL YOU BE ABLE TO DEVELOP A STRATEGY FOR THE SALE.

PICKING YOUR KNOWLEDGE CALL CONTACTS

You can and should request a Knowledge Call with almost any contact—from a person you've never met who represents a company that your own firm has never done business with, to a longtime contact at a well-established account. In selecting contacts for Knowledge Calls, follow these guidelines:

1. **A true coach is by far your best Knowledge Call contact.** Remember, coaches are more than "friendly contacts." Coaches want you to have an advantage over your competition. They give you information that they wouldn't give your competitors. Just beware the ubiquitous friendly gatekeeper masquerading as a coach.

2. **Start with the least powerful, most talkative people first.** This is the best way to avoid gatekeepers who try to block your ascent. It's also how you prepare yourself as you move to more powerful contacts in the customer company.

3. **If it's an existing customer, start with your day-to-day contacts.** Just be alert to a tendency on the part of some contacts to act as gatekeepers. Sometimes you're stuck with a contact whom you might otherwise not have chosen.

4. **Never attempt a Knowledge Call with someone who might be considered "off limits."** Secretaries fall into this category. With any prospective Knowledge Call contact, ask yourself if there's any chance that your contact—or any others in the company—might get the impression, even if mistakenly, that you're snooping.

5. **Former employees/nonemployees.** Depending on your relationship with them and their relationship with the targeted company, such individuals can be buried treasure. Tony discovered this when he snagged Mike, a new contact at one account who, coincidentally, had only weeks earlier left another of Tony's key customers. Their forty-five-minute Knowledge Call turned into two hours and gave Tony the insight he needed to save a $250,000 deal that was being torpedoed by someone working for Mike's former employer.

6. **When your initial entry to an account is through an executive, and you have no good lower-level contacts, make a "mini–Knowledge Call" part of your introductory meeting with the executive.** Contrary to popular selling notions, it's a bad idea to do Knowledge Calls with senior executives, as you'll see in Chapter 6. However, when your first meeting at an account is with an executive, you should ask a few high-level, strategic questions as part of that meeting. But never try to conduct the

same kind of in-depth Knowledge Call that you would with a good coach.

A KNOWLEDGE CALL MUST BE POSITIONED, NOT JUST REQUESTED

The first step in conducting a Knowledge Call is, of course, to request the meeting, and when doing so, positioning is everything. Thus, your request involves far more than simply scheduling time together. It doesn't matter if you've never met the person with whom you're attempting to schedule a Knowledge Call, or if you've called on that person for years. *Every request for a Knowledge Call must be positioned, without exception.*

In many cases, how you position the call determines whether or not you even get the meeting. But it's also a major factor in determining how the meeting actually goes. A Knowledge Call positioned incorrectly or without sufficient clarity can set the salesperson up for a disaster. Keep in mind a basic formula: "Expectations minus reality equals stress." Customers don't expect Knowledge Calls. They expect sales calls.

Cory, the sales rep whose Knowledge Call was so successful that his contact actually embraced him, had paid close attention to positioning when he telephoned John to set up their appointment.

"I think I've got a pretty good handle on the day-to-day issues at your company, but I'm not certain that I've kept up with your company's more strategic issues," Cory began. "Perhaps we could schedule a different kind of meeting," he continued. "I'd leave the traditional discussion we might have for another time so I can dedicate my effort to understanding your business and your organization."

As you position your own Knowledge Calls, consider the following:

1. **What is your own personal, past relationship with the contact?** If, at one end of the spectrum, you've never met the person, your positioning would naturally have

EVERY REQUEST FOR A KNOWLEDGE CALL MUST BE POSITIONED, WITHOUT EXCEPTION.

to reflect that absence of a relationship. Nonetheless, requesting a Knowledge Call with a new contact is by no means inappropriate.

Don't become preoccupied with "building rapport" with your contact, as if that were some sort of self-imposed prerequisite to asking for a Knowledge Call. Your primary objective is for you and the contact to get to know each other as business peers, not as buddies. Frankly, most of the better contacts have little time for excessive rapport-building.

Besides, what better way to quickly establish yourself as a Business Resource than to conduct an effective, business-issues-driven Knowledge Call during your first meeting? Naturally, you will spend a little more time in warming up with someone you don't already know, but it isn't necessary to dedicate an entire meeting just to getting to know each other.

Of course, if the new contact is not familiar with your company, you'll have to spend a minute positioning your company and the potential value it can provide. But don't belabor this discussion, or you will defeat the Knowledge Call's intent and get sucked into a traditional needs/solutions discussion.

At the other end of the spectrum is the contact with whom you have a long-standing relationship. Positioning a Knowledge Call under those circumstances should actually be easier than where there is no relationship at all. Nevertheless, salespeople often worry, "Won't I look silly after having called on this person for a few years on a regular basis to now tell him that I don't know anything about his business?" The answer is yes, you will—absolutely—if that's how you position your request for the meeting.

On the other hand, you'll get a much better reception if you position your request in a way that acknowledges that you've been doing business together for a long

WHAT BETTER WAY TO QUICKLY ESTABLISH YOURSELF AS A BUSINESS RESOURCE THAN TO CONDUCT AN EFFECTIVE, BUSINESS-ISSUES-DRIVEN KNOWLEDGE CALL DURING YOUR FIRST MEETING?

time—and that you want to make sure your focus in the relationship with this customer continues to center on bringing business value.

Simply point out to the contact, "It's been quite some time since we've had a meeting where we attempted to leave the day-to-day discussions at the door. It's time to take a step back and go into homework mode." This is one of the most effective ways to move yourself from the Problem-Solver level to the Business Resource level in the eyes of an existing customer.

2. **What is your company's past relationship with the contact?** How you position a Knowledge Call should also reflect your company's past relationship with that account. The wording you use to position a Knowledge Call at a firm with which your company has a long-standing relationship is quite different from the wording you use to position such a call with a customer who has no existing relationship with your company.

3. **Word choice and style are critical.** Keep your wording informal, casual, and conversational, not stuffy, sterile, or formal. One of the words that seems to drive home best what it is you're trying to do is "homework." By contrast, one word that tends to spook customers is "information," as in, "We're trying to get more information on your company." Predictably, the customer responds, "What kind of information are you looking for?"

"We're trying to better understand your business" is more productive than "We're trying to learn about it." You might try saying "We were hoping you could share your insights with us" as opposed to "We wanted to ask you some questions." If the person you're talking to is someone you're certain could be a good coach for you, use words such as "guidance" and "direction"—not "help," which conveys a message of "I need you to do my selling for me."

While many details of how you position a Knowledge Call vary depending on your situation, all Knowledge Call requests have one important quality that should come through clearly: sincerity. You have to believe that your request for this call is not some kind of sales gimmick. You're requesting this Knowledge Call because you sincerely believe that the better you understand your customer's business, the more value you can bring to that customer.

In other words, you must believe that a Knowledge Call is a mutually beneficial activity—because it *is*. If you believe its purpose is only that of the customer helping you sell to his or her company, you've missed the point.

As you position the call, you need to engage in a careful balancing act—on the one hand, clearly conveying that the meeting will be different from a typical sales call, on the other, avoiding any impression that the call is a major event or some form of snooping.

With these thoughts in mind, here are some words to *avoid,* no matter what the intended context, any time you're positioning a Knowledge Call:

- "talk" (sounds too much like you'll be doing the talking)
- "discuss" (also sounds too much like you'll be doing the talking)
- "information" (usually elicits the response, "What kind of information are you looking for?")
- "tell" (even if you say, "Perhaps you could tell me about . . . " the contact usually hears, "I'd like to tell you about . . . .")
- "explore" (sounds like "needs assessment")
- "needs" (clearly says "needs assessment")
- "interview" (sounds too structured and formal)
- "survey" (I know you'd never use this word, but just in case)
- "confidential" (prompts a thought in the customer's mind, "I'm about to be asked stuff I shouldn't be talking about")

> YOU MUST BELIEVE THAT A KNOWLEDGE CALL IS A MUTUALLY BENEFICIAL ACTIVITY—BECAUSE IT *IS.* IF YOU BELIEVE ITS PURPOSE IS ONLY THAT OF THE CUSTOMER HELPING YOU SELL TO HIS OR HER COMPANY, YOU'VE MISSED THE POINT.

- "ask" (hard to separate from "ask you some questions," which usually prompts the response, "What kinds of questions are you going to ask me?")

- "research" (tends to have a million connotations, none of which is favorable to positioning a Knowledge Call)

- "Knowledge Call" (triggers the thought, "What training program did you just get out of?")

Here are a few proven phrases that work under a number of circumstances:

- "We believe the better we understand your business, the more value we can bring you." (Remember: "business," not "needs")

- "I'd like to go into homework mode."

- "I feel I know the day-to-day issues pretty well."

- "I'd like to get a better handle on the big picture."

- "I'd like to gain a better understanding."

- "I'll leave the products at the door."

- "I'd like to take a step back."

If you want to calibrate your success rate at positioning Knowledge Calls, consider this as a standard: In the countless Knowledge Calls that I and my firm's consultants have conducted with clients, which cover a wide range of industries, personalities, relationship history, and so on, over 90 percent of all requests for Knowledge Calls result in an affirmative response from the customer.

If your own success rate, after you've gone through the learning curve, is significantly less than this, you should conclude that some nuance—usually just one—needs adjusting. I urge you not to conclude that your situation is different.

> OVER **90** PERCENT OF ALL REQUESTS FOR **KNOWLEDGE CALLS** RESULT IN AN AFFIRMATIVE RESPONSE FROM THE CUSTOMER.

CONTROL YOUR KNOWLEDGE CALL LOGISTICS

You must take ownership of controlling the logistics of the meeting. Here are some pointers:

Don't "do lunch." The Knowledge Call is a business meeting and therefore should be held in a business setting. The question is frequently asked, "Wouldn't lunch be a great place to do a Knowledge Call?" The answer is "No," for a couple of reasons.

Lunch carries an expectation of being primarily social and secondarily business. Trying to conduct an intensive Knowledge Call over lunch is, at best, clumsy. You can't possibly expect to get any momentum going in the call, since you'll frequently be interrupted by the waitstaff. Also, it's not easy to take notes while dining.

Another reason that lunch is a bad setting for a Knowledge Call is one of confidentiality. Although you're not trying to get information about a company that shouldn't be shared with you, it's not a public discussion, either. And just as a practical matter, you never know who is sitting at the next table. If your contact is a "lunch customer," schedule the Knowledge Call at 10:30 or 11:00 A.M. and plan to go to lunch afterwards. You can use the lunch meeting to fill in the gaps you may have overlooked during the meeting itself.

One at a time. Knowledge Calls are best when only one customer contact is involved at a time. You're not looking for information that the customer shouldn't tell you, yet at the same time you are trying to better understand some of the organizational dynamics. Most people are not as comfortable talking about those kinds of things if a coworker is part of the meeting. So if you are hoping to conduct a Knowledge Call with several people at a particular company, try to schedule them as separate meetings.

As you attempt to schedule Knowledge Calls, you may find that getting to meet with only one contact at a time can be difficult. Remember, for generations customers have been conditioned by salespeople to behave in certain ways. One of these behaviors is to spontaneously, and often without any particular reason, get others involved when a vendor comes to visit. Customers usually do this with the best

FOR GENERATIONS CUSTOMERS HAVE BEEN CONDITIONED BY SALESPEOPLE TO BEHAVE IN CERTAIN WAYS. ONE OF THESE BEHAVIORS IS TO SPONTANEOUSLY, AND OFTEN WITHOUT ANY PARTICULAR REASON, GET OTHERS INVOLVED WHEN A VENDOR COMES TO VISIT.

of intentions, reasoning that you, the salesperson, would like as many eyes and ears as possible to receive your pitch.

My experience with my clients' salespeople is that they eventually crack the wording code when positioning Knowledge Calls so that unexpected occurrences become the exception. However, sometimes you are not able to avoid having multiple people attend a Knowledge Call. When that happens, accept it, but also lower your expectations for the outcome.

One final point. The ideal number of people representing the salesperson's company is two. Three can work, but that starts to look like "an event." One of you is obviously fine, too.

Quiet, please. A quiet, private setting is the best location for a Knowledge Call. If the client contact has an office, that will usually do. On the other hand, if the person lives in cubesville, move to a conference room. In fact, when you're scheduling the call, it's better if you know in advance whether the person works out of a cube so you can suggest getting a conference room.

When you show up for the Knowledge Call, if you are taken to the contact's cube, take the small chance of annoying the customer by suggesting—before you even sit down—a move to a conference room. Remember, you are steering the sales campaign, and customers like it when you do.

PREPARE FOR THE KNOWLEDGE CALL

Before actually conducting the Knowledge Call, it's essential that you do all the homework you reasonably can. Few things are more awkward than starting a Knowledge Call by having your contact hand you a copy of the company's annual report with all the company information that you should have known before the meeting—or telling you during the call, "Most of this is on our Web site."

As I've said, there is no comprehensive list of Knowledge Call questions, nor could there be. A Knowledge Call is not

SOMETIMES YOU ARE NOT ABLE TO AVOID HAVING MULTIPLE PEOPLE ATTEND A KNOWLEDGE CALL. WHEN THAT HAPPENS, ACCEPT IT, BUT ALSO LOWER YOUR EXPECTATIONS FOR THE OUTCOME.

a survey, and nothing could seem more insincere and contrived than to go into a Knowledge Call with a prepared list of questions. You are trying to understand a customer company from a business and organizational perspective. Your questions should reflect that desire.

CONDUCT THE KNOWLEDGE CALL

You've finally arrived at the customer's office, and you're ready to start the Knowledge Call. This doesn't require fancy skills, but it does demand discipline. Keep several things in mind as the call progresses:

1. **Recognize that a Knowledge Call has a tone all its own.** A Knowledge Call is conversational and informal, yet business-oriented and focused. It's unstructured, yet organized. Consider what a Knowledge Call *isn't* so you can best capture that unique "Knowledge Call tone."

   A Knowledge Call should never come down as:

   - a vaguely positioned information-gathering meeting
   - a survey
   - a needs assessment
   - an interrogation
   - espionage
   - an interview
   - fact-finding
   - research
   - snooping
   - a "sales" call
   - random listening

   By contrast, here are some things that describe what the atmosphere of a Knowledge Call *should* be:

   - clearly positioned
   - steered by the salesperson
   - comfortable, conversational, informal
   - seemingly unstructured

- of mutual value

- a business meeting

A good way to summarize this atmosphere is "above-board/under the radar," meaning that you are clear about what your purpose is for the meeting (above-board) while having it viewed as a minor occurrence (under the radar).

2. **Warm up the contact to an appropriate level.** Sometimes that appropriate level involves no warm-up at all, because you know, either from experience or from on-the-spot observation, that this person prefers to get right to the point. But it's still risky to avoid some amount of warm-up at the beginning of a Knowledge Call, however brief.

   By contrast, certain contacts require a lot of warm-up time, with talk about sports and other peripheral subjects, before getting into the heart of the meeting. Gauge what's appropriate, and allow enough time for warm-up as the situation warrants.

3. **Clearly position the meeting—no matter what!** At the right moment it's critical to move seamlessly but definitively from warming up the contact into positioning the meeting—that is, setting a clear direction for the meeting.

   Such positioning almost always begins, "Jack, as I mentioned on the phone . . . ," and repeat the same wording you used when you first set up the meeting.

   Even if the contact gets ahead of you and begins to discuss the company and where it's going before you can clearly position the meeting, you must look for a spot to jump in and do so—without killing the momentum.

   One really useful tip: Don't start to take notes until after you've done this positioning.

   It can be a formula for disaster to allow a Knowledge Call to simply drift from warm-up into the call itself.

IT CAN BE A FORMULA FOR DISASTER TO ALLOW A KNOWLEDGE CALL TO SIMPLY DRIFT FROM WARM-UP INTO THE CALL ITSELF.

What can happen is that several minutes into the call the contact abruptly asks, with a trace of annoyance, "So, where are you going with all this?" At best, the contact fails to fully appreciate the purpose of your questions—meaning that you fail to score those valuable "Business Resource points" that a properly positioned Knowledge Call makes possible.

I repeat: You must clearly restate the direction you want to take with the meeting early in the call, no matter how clearly you might have done so when you set it up originally or how receptive your contact might have been to the idea at that time.

> **YOU MUST CLEARLY RESTATE THE DIRECTION YOU WANT TO TAKE WITH THE MEETING EARLY IN THE CALL, NO MATTER HOW CLEARLY YOU MIGHT HAVE DONE SO WHEN YOU SET IT UP ORIGINALLY.**

Before moving ahead, it's a good idea to check for any urgent issues that might be on the customer's mind. One of my clients won't ever forget the time that he spared his own backside (and mine) by doing this. We aborted a Knowledge Call in favor of a product discussion once we discovered, by way of this quick reality check, what was really on the contact's mind. She hammered us with her frustration that someone else at my client's company still hadn't gotten back to her with product information she urgently needed for a meeting the next day. If we hadn't given her that chance, we would have been toast.

After experiencing a reaction like that a few times, you learn very quickly how critically important it is to set a clear direction at the start of the Knowledge Call. Here's one way to flush out issues and get a read on how receptive the contact is to the direction you're planning to take. At the end of your positioning of the call, say something such as, "So, that's the direction we're hoping to go in this meeting. Make sense to you?" Then, after only a slight pause, add something to this effect: "Having said that, do you have any pressing issues that you want to make sure we discuss while we're together today?"

If the contact responds in the affirmative, either get her issue out of the way immediately or ask if you could circle back to it before leaving. Whatever you do, just make it clear that you're going to address her issue.

4. **Avoid any references to confidentiality.** By bringing up confidentiality, you make it an issue where it would not otherwise exist. You should also be sensitive to moments when the contact confides in you before telling you something—as, for instance, by saying, "You know, you didn't hear it here," or "Don't repeat this, but . . . ." When that happens, you must put down your pen. At other times the customer won't say directly that he's talking about a confidential subject, but you'll notice that he begins speaking much more quietly, indicating that he doesn't want coworkers to overhear what he's saying. In that case, stop writing.

5. **Avoid overstructuring or formalizing the Knowledge Call.** Don't go in with a list of questions. Your customer will wonder what sales training program you just came out of. Keep your language informal, light, and conversational. Aim for a lively discussion, not a structured survey.

   Most Knowledge Calls jump frequently from one topic to the next—say, from the customer's business to the customer's organization—and back again. This is normal. It usually indicates that the meeting has that Knowledge Call tone.

6. **Practice Business Resource listening, not Vendor/Problem-Solver listening.** None of us is as good at listening as we think we are. And listening is certainly not a virtue for which salespeople are generally well known. At best, we're listening only for an opportunity to sell the customer something.

   Of course, there's another aspect to Vendor/Problem-Solver listening that I refer to as "mindless listening."

MOST KNOWLEDGE CALLS JUMP FREQUENTLY FROM ONE TOPIC TO THE NEXT—SAY, FROM THE CUSTOMER'S BUSINESS TO THE CUSTOMER'S ORGANIZATION—AND BACK AGAIN. THIS IS NORMAL. IT USUALLY INDICATES THAT THE MEETING HAS THAT KNOWLEDGE CALL TONE.

Some salespeople, armed with a newfound awareness that they should listen, simply let the contact yak away, believing that they're doing what they're supposed to be doing.

Learn to be an "active listener." Let the customer "hear" you listening from your "uh-huhs." Follow the 90/10 rule, with the customer talking 90 percent of the time and you talking 10 percent of the time. Process the contact's comments, pause, and ask a follow-up question. Engage the contact! This process is the reason that a typical Knowledge Call, unlike most sales calls, tends to go much longer than you or the customer had scheduled. Of course, extending the time occurs only at the customer's prompting.

> **A TYPICAL KNOWLEDGE CALL, UNLIKE MOST SALES CALLS, TENDS TO GO MUCH LONGER THAN YOU OR THE CUSTOMER HAD SCHEDULED.**

7. **Ask the contact challenging questions.** You'll become known for the kinds of questions you ask. If you merely lob in softball questions, you are not going to be viewed as a Business Resource. Although it's a good idea to open the Knowledge Call with questions that are easy for the contact to answer, you want to move from there to asking your best, most insightful questions. Exercise your strategic sense of curiosity.

8. **Get comfortable with dead air.** We sales professionals do not like silence. Fortunately, that's true of most people. When you ask a question that's hard for the contact to answer immediately, don't take her off the hook. Let her think about her response for awhile. You have to become comfortable with the dead air that might result. The contact is likely to be drawn to fill the silence, often with very useful information. Moreover, you will get credit for asking insightful questions.

9. **Ask questions in an interesting way.** I once heard an interview with musician Jimmy Buffett. One of the many good questions the interviewer asked went much like this: "If you were to lock yourself into, say, Carnegie Hall, with no fans, no audience of any kind,

just you and your music, would you play 'Margarita-ville'? 'Cheeseburger in Paradise'?"

Some salespeople might say, "That's not a good question because it's closed-ended. We should be asking open-ended questions." Okay, here's an open-ended version of that same question: "Jimmy, what are your favorite songs?" Which do you think is the better way to interest someone and gain a rich response?

When you're on a Knowledge Call, don't ask, by way of example, "What are the VP's goals?" Try something such as, "If I were a fly on the wall during one of the VP's staff meetings, what initiatives, projects, priorities, or issues would I likely hear about as he goes around the room asking the members of his staff what's happening?"

By asking questions in an interesting way, you prove yourself a skilled professional and elicit much richer responses.

10. **Take notes**! What better way is there to demonstrate that you mean business? Taking notes sends the message to the customer that you're serious about this. It can even be somewhat flattering. Remember, don't start writing any notes until you've positioned the call.

11. **Watch the time.** When the allotted time is upon you, use a phrase such as, "I want to be mindful of the time. I've noticed that our forty-five minutes are up." Usually you don't have to say much more to get a good read from the customer. More often than not, the customer tells you to continue with the meeting.

12. **Suggest a next step.** When it is time to close the meeting, don't do it by acknowledging how important the customer's time is. Don't say, "I know how busy you must be," or "I'll let you get back to work." That's classic Vendor language. It sends a message that you're wasting the customer's time, as if he or she is doing you a favor by "granting" you the meeting. If that were the case, the contact shouldn't be meeting with you at all.

BY ASKING QUESTIONS IN AN INTERESTING WAY, YOU PROVE YOURSELF A SKILLED PROFESSIONAL AND ELICIT MUCH RICHER RESPONSES.

DON'T SAY, "I KNOW HOW BUSY YOU MUST BE," OR "I'LL LET YOU GET BACK TO WORK." THAT'S CLASSIC VENDOR LANGUAGE.

Instead, express gratitude for the meeting, pause for a second to analyze everything that you've talked about, then suggest a next step. Don't ask the contact what she thinks you should do next.

Just what that next step is depends on how your contact has reacted to the Knowledge Call itself. Quickly and accurately size up the session in your own mind. Do you sense your contact is something of a gatekeeper whose job is to keep you away from others? If so, this is one of the few times when you might want to keep the next step vague. You don't want to give her an opportunity to exercise that power and keep you away from other contacts at the customer company, including executives.

At the opposite extreme, perhaps this contact demonstrates a strongly favorable view of you and of your company and is very open to the idea of your returning to make a Business Presentation to senior management. Then your close can suggest that such a presentation seems like an appropriate next step. It might even offer an opportunity to enlist the contact to help set up such a meeting.

13. **Confirm future access.** This may seem unnecessary, especially for customers with whom you've had a relationship for a while. Confirming such access is helpful more as a barometer of how the meeting has gone. Simply ask the customer contact if it's okay to contact him again if you need to clarify a few things. The answer will give you a good sense of his receptivity to the call itself. This step also helps you avoid a situation in which you call the contact on the phone a week later to clarify some things and he replies, "Gee, didn't we already cover all that stuff?"

CONDUCTING A KNOWLEDGE CALL BY PHONE

Phone-based Knowledge Calls might be the most under-leveraged tool in selling. Virtually all the rules that apply to

---

DO YOU SENSE YOUR CONTACT IS SOMETHING OF A GATEKEEPER WHOSE JOB IS TO KEEP YOU AWAY FROM OTHERS? IF SO, THIS IS ONE OF THE FEW TIMES WHEN YOU MIGHT WANT TO KEEP THE NEXT STEP VAGUE.

a face-to-face Knowledge Call apply as well to a telephone Knowledge Call. One obvious difference is that you can't read body language, an important part of the total communication process. During a Knowledge Call, body language is a good indicator of what the customer is feeling about the call. However, you'll quickly see that contacts signal their receptivity—or lack of it—in other ways over the phone.

Telephone Knowledge Calls are most appropriate under the following circumstances:

- when there isn't time to conduct a face-to-face Knowledge Call before some impending event, such as a presentation to an executive;

- when you believe that the person with whom you want to conduct a Knowledge Call has a limited amount of knowledge that he or she is able to share with you or would be willing to, thus making a face-to-face call unproductive or not cost-effective;

- when you currently have only one contact and are trying to get a better feel for the organization so you can make more face-to-face Knowledge Calls when you eventually go on site;

- when the perceived opportunity doesn't warrant the expense of a face-to-face meeting;

- when you're still trying to determine how real or how good the perceived opportunity is.

The most important thing about a telephone Knowledge Call, like its face-to-face counterpart, is to position it, never allowing yourself to just start asking questions and see how it goes.

SEEK, AND YOU SHALL FIND

If selling were a car, the Knowledge Call would be the engine that powers it. In the absence of Knowledge Calls, even the slickest form of traditional selling would be like a Ferrari with a Yugo engine—it would look good but not move you along very well.

THE MOST IMPORTANT THING ABOUT A TELEPHONE KNOWLEDGE CALL, LIKE ITS FACE-TO-FACE COUNTERPART, IS TO POSITION IT, NEVER ALLOWING YOURSELF TO JUST START ASKING QUESTIONS AND SEE HOW IT GOES.

In the new era of selling, salespeople are not able to bring value to customers the old-fashioned way—by communicating information. Product knowledge and technical expertise—the engine of the "old car"—will not power the vehicle of the future. And as the cliché goes, the future truly is now.

Don't underestimate the value of operating in seek mode or the difficulty you are most likely to have in doing so. Evolution has taught salespeople to operate in tell mode. Changing modes takes more than just flipping a switch.

EVOLUTION HAS TAUGHT SALESPEOPLE TO OPERATE IN TELL MODE. CHANGING MODES TAKES MORE THAN JUST FLIPPING A SWITCH.

chapter 4

"Being powerful is like being a lady. If you have to tell people you are, you aren't."

—Margaret Thatcher

HOW ORGANIZATIONS *REALLY* WORK

FORGET "FINDING THE DECISION-MAKER"—BECOME ORGANIZATIONALLY SAVVY

Helen sells for a Fortune 500 company, a leading supplier of software and equipment for processing credit card transactions. Let's call the firm Beta Company. For the last year or so, AlphaCard, a longtime customer of Beta, has been one of Helen's key accounts.

Beta recently developed a significant new advance in credit card processing software, a development so new that none of its competitors had comparable solutions. Ralph, Beta's regional vice president of sales and Helen's boss, thought he sniffed an opportunity. He pushed Helen to set up a meeting with Jim, AlphaCard's vice president of operations. "Get in there and talk to the vice president," Ralph said. "Anybody can see how advanced our new software is. We've got to get it in front of the decision-maker before the folks over at ZetaSoft (Beta's competitor) come up with their own version."

But Helen held Ralph off. He became a little annoyed—it was so obvious, he thought, that she should strike while the iron was hot. It was all Helen could do to stay firm in her conviction that the time was not as ripe as Ralph thought.

Indeed, Helen had good reason for biding her time. Over the last few months, she had been doing her homework. In particular, she had learned that AlphaCard was in the throes of change since hiring a new president one year before. Helen learned from her contacts that AlphaCard's board had recruited its president from IBM, and—as one contact put it—given him marching orders to "tear down the silos, kill the country-club atmosphere, and return the company to profitability."

Helen wasn't just absorbing random gossip. She was putting into practice her organizational savvy. She well knew that her new solution had to do more than make technical or business sense for AlphaCard—it had to make *political* sense. She observed, analyzed, and asked careful questions. As a result, she was able to piece together the political dynamics. Slowly, one by one, the new president had been quietly replacing most of AlphaCard's senior management team with people of his own choosing— mostly people he brought over from IBM.

Further complicating the picture, most of the original people being replaced kept their jobs, and often their titles. Those who had big offices kept those, too. Only on very close inspection could one see that these incumbents had lost the lion's share of the influence they had wielded a year earlier.

That was why Helen didn't run to Jim, AlphaCard's vice president of operations, with a sales pitch for Beta's new software package. Yes, Jim had been with AlphaCard for many years, and most of the company's employees worked under him. His was arguably the most strategic department in the company. And AlphaCard's operations department was also the key end user of Beta's new software. Certainly, any decision to commit considerable financial resources to Helen's software package would require the support of whoever headed that department. But everything Helen heard and saw of the changes

SHE WELL KNEW THAT HER NEW SOLUTION HAD TO DO MORE THAN MAKE TECHNICAL OR BUSINESS SENSE FOR ALPHACARD—IT HAD TO MAKE *POLITICAL* SENSE.

underway at AlphaCard convinced her that Jim would not be the person to woo.

"Let's wait a month or so," she told Ralph. "I want to see what other moves the president makes." She explained her hunch that Jim would soon be history.

Ralph was now more than annoyed! He was under pressure from Beta's management for results. But he also knew that Helen was one of the best on his team, so very reluctantly, he agreed to trust her instincts.

He was glad he did. Six weeks after Ralph's discussion with Helen, Jim was reassigned to the post of VP of special projects, with a total of two people reporting to him. Replacing him as AlphaCard's VP of operations was Ed, an executive recruited from IBM.

Helen went from biding her time to taking action. Within two weeks, she was in front of Ed, positioning Beta Corp.'s new software development. She knew it wasn't merely the superiority of the new product that would win the sale for Beta. Ed, she knew, would see in the deal an opportunity to quickly add a feather to his cap in his new position at AlphaCard.

OLD CLICHÉS DIE HARD

There is probably no more universally accepted, dogmatic rule in selling than "find the decision-maker!" Yet if you're going to succeed as a new era salesperson, you'd better be prepared to jettison this outdated cliché.

For years, I have been exhorting salespeople to avoid this overly simplistic approach to figuring out who's who in their customer organizations. My mantra has always been that "decision-maker" is a meaningless term; instead, *seek to become organizationally savvy*. This is a difficult pill for most salespeople to swallow. Only a small minority tried. Even fewer achieved it.

But it's no longer optional; only those salespeople who become organizationally savvy will succeed in the redefined business of selling.

THERE IS PROBABLY NO MORE UNIVERSALLY ACCEPTED, DOGMATIC RULE IN SELLING THAN "FIND THE DECISION-MAKER!" YET IF YOU'RE GOING TO SUCCEED AS A NEW ERA SALESPERSON, YOU'D BETTER BE PREPARED TO JETTISON THIS OUTDATED CLICHÉ.

In this chapter, I tell you why and how.

Helen's experience shows what happens when organizational savvy is applied to a sales campaign. Would you have done what she did—ask the questions, extrapolate from the little information she had that Jim was on his way out, and wait patiently? Or would you have moved blindly toward a meeting with Jim on the strength of his VP title, like her boss wanted her to do, and, in this case, toward certain defeat?

Although many of you might like to say you would have done what she did, my own experience as player/coach accompanying thousands of salespeople in live sales situations tells me that only a small fraction of them would have had the insight, or the guts, to pursue Helen's wait-and-listen strategy.

Consider another case. Frank is a major account sales executive for ABC Chemical, one of the largest chemical companies in the world. Among Frank's most promising prospects is XYZ Ltd., one of the largest manufacturers in Canada. After nearly a year spent cultivating this prospect, Frank won an opportunity to make a presentation to the Canadian firm's president.

Frank sweated over the details. He steeped himself in everything he could learn about XYZ: its markets, its competition, and the trends in its industry. He put together a Business Presentation demonstrating a compelling fit between the two companies, rehearsed it thoroughly, and brought along one of ABC Chemical's own senior executives.

On the appointed day, Frank, his immediate manager, and the ABC senior executive met with XYZ's president. Frank conducted his presentation. The results were astounding, even to him. XYZ's president agreed to all of his recommendations, and the two companies proceeded toward what in just a few weeks would be the biggest sale Frank ever made.

But it never got that far. Two weeks after Frank's presentation, XYZ's president was summarily fired by the

MY OWN EXPERIENCE AS PLAYER/COACH ACCOMPANYING THOUSANDS OF SALESPEOPLE IN LIVE SALES SITUATIONS TELLS ME THAT ONLY A SMALL FRACTION OF THEM WOULD HAVE HAD THE INSIGHT, OR THE GUTS, TO PURSUE HELEN'S WAIT-AND-LISTEN STRATEGY.

CEO, replaced almost immediately by the vice president for operations—someone Frank had never included in his selling efforts. The sale fizzled; Frank, who had already begun spending the commission money he was so sure he would receive, lost the biggest opportunity of his life because he made the mistake of assuming that the company's president was influential—which is usually, but not always, a safe assumption.

What Helen has, and Frank lacks, is organizational savvy: an understanding of the ebb and flow of power and influence in the customer organizations with which they are dealing.

Consider yet a third case. Lisa, a veteran financial software salesperson, just sold a huge deal to the chief financial officer at one of her key accounts. A week into the installation of the software, a very embarrassed and apologetic CFO called Lisa with the stunningly bad news that his company had decided not to buy the software after all and would instead de-install what had already been installed. It seems the chief information officer, who hadn't been very involved in the buying process, killed the deal, not an uncommon occurrence in technology-related sales.

The shocking news to Lisa was this: the chief information officer reported to the CFO. The CIO had cited some esoteric technical issue for rejecting the software, but it struck Lisa as clearly fabricated to sanitize his own political agenda.

What makes this case even more unusual is that the purchase in question was financial software. Who should be more influential on such a purchase than a company's CFO? And then to be upstaged by a subordinate, no less? What's wrong with this picture?

Lisa was at a loss. When she related the story to me, the situation was still warm. So I gave her a few questions to go back and ask her lower-level contacts about the three players. The bottom line: the CFO had been with Lisa's target company twenty years. The president had been

ORGANIZATIONAL SAVVY: AN UNDERSTANDING OF THE EBB AND FLOW OF POWER AND INFLUENCE IN THE CUSTOMER ORGANIZATION

hired only a year ago. The CIO had been hired six months after the president, having come from the same company. This information was critical to the outcome of the sale, but Lisa had not bothered asking the right questions early in the sales cycle. She had relied, like most salespeople, on the strong "solution fit" and on the title of the executive buying her financial software—the CFO.

Most Salespeople Lack Organizational Savvy

Extreme examples? Not at all. Such episodes occur every day in a salesperson's world. Every sales cycle is profoundly influenced by political factors, whether we like it or not. Salespeople must remember that in the real world of corporate life, political reasons trump business reasons for any decision, including a buying decision.

That's why organizational savvy is arguably the single most important competency required for successful selling to large, complex accounts. Unfortunately, it's probably the single most common deficiency shared by people selling to these same accounts.

It's an unfortunate reality that most salespeople are weakest at the thing that contributes the most to their success. Worse, they suffer from unconscious incompetence—they don't know what they don't know. Most salespeople—dare I say—naively believe that a customer's formal organizational chart and an individual's title are the only things they need worry about in determining who the so-called "key decision-makers" are.

One reason so many salespeople fall short in their organizational savvy is that they have not spent much time actually working inside a company, where they can see close up how power and influence work within corporations. This is not merely accidental. They have been drawn to sales, in part, because for all of their stereotypical garrulousness, many salespeople are loners at heart who like the freedom and distance from the home office that their trade provides.

> SALESPEOPLE MUST REMEMBER THAT IN THE REAL WORLD OF CORPORATE LIFE, POLITICAL REASONS TRUMP BUSINESS REASONS FOR ANY DECISION, INCLUDING A BUYING DECISION.

A second reason is closely related. Salespeople who have worked for a while on the inside of a company very likely started out in some other position. Few launch their careers planning to be salespeople. Among the reasons they often cite for later transferring into sales sounds something like "being tired of all the political BS at corporate."

In group sessions on this topic with salespeople, I like to play a word association game. Their responses to the word "politics" are almost invariably negative, conveying images of Machiavellian maneuvering, backbiting, and the like.

I recently saw a cartoon in which two men in business suits were dueling with swords in the hallway of what was clearly a big corporate office. Two observers stood off to the side. Said one, "I don't get involved in office politics."

That's not what I mean when I talk about understanding a customer's political structure. I'm referring to learning where the real power lies within any company. This chapter discusses power and influence, not the dark side of office politics. The words "dirty" and "politics" are not always connected.

THIS CHAPTER DISCUSSES POWER AND INFLUENCE, NOT THE DARK SIDE OF OFFICE POLITICS. THE WORDS "DIRTY" AND "POLITICS" ARE NOT ALWAYS CONNECTED.

HOW TO IDENTIFY INFLUENCE IN ANY COMPANY, NEW ERA OR OLD

In this "blur economy" in which we now live, the notion of a fixed, hierarchical organizational structure is as much an anachronism as the blue suit uniform at IBM. Whether you accept the term "New Economy" or not, it's an inescapable reality that people come and go at companies with lightning speed. Even "the company" itself can be ephemeral, being quickly absorbed by another organization or morphing into a newer version of itself. Titles are disappearing, too. What's a salesperson to do?

Consider the following remarks by Avram Miller, former vice president and director of business development at Intel Corporation, reported in the December 1999 *Fast Company* magazine:

Corporations are becoming less important. The Internet is made up of companies that pop up, live for a while, and get absorbed. Take, for example, broadcast.com, a four-year-old company that Yahoo! bought for roughly $5.2 billion.

It used to be that people would join a corporation with the expectation not only that they would spend their whole career there but also that their sons and daughters would go to work for the company, and that the company would live forever. Now companies have a shorter life expectancy than a California marriage. Not only do you not expect to spend your whole career at one company, but the company might disappear before you leave it. You don't even have to change jobs to change jobs.

Or consider the words of management icon Peter Drucker, reported in *Business 2.0.*

The corporation as we know it, which is now 120 years old, is unlikely to survive the next 25 years. Legally and financially, yes, but not structurally and economically.

THAT'S WHY IT'S SO TERRIBLY IMPORTANT THAT THE SALES REPS IN THIS NEW ERA OF SELLING FORGET OLD NOTIONS ABOUT FINDING THE "DECISION-MAKER."

That's why it's so terribly important that the sales reps in this new era of selling forget old notions about finding the "decision-maker." They must even move deeper than trying to identify the "buying roles"—economic buyer, user buyer, and the like. Organizational savvy, once a tool possessed by only a few elite salespeople, is now a basic survival tool.

New era or old, bricks-and-mortar company or virtual one, big organization or small, what determines how things get done and decisions get made is politics—power and influence. The language of politics may change, but the existence and importance of politics never does.

So how do power and influence really work? Where does power come from? How does one get it, keep it, and use it? And how do you, as a sales professional, identify it and make sure that the true power players are on your side?

At least in the past, salespeople had a formal organizational structure to provide guidance in understanding who was powerful and who was not. To be sure, most made the mistake of simply assuming that the higher a person was on the organizational chart, the more powerful that person was. Still, it was a starting point. With today's often amorphous structures (an oxymoron, I know), it gets even harder.

For you, perhaps the hardest part of this perspective is acknowledging that you probably have been making erroneous assumptions about who is truly powerful in your accounts. After all, what salesperson wants to think he's calling on lightweights? Yet the very nature of power, as I show you in these pages, predicts that the people you're calling on are often less powerful within their own organizations than you think. It's a truism in selling that the contacts with the least power are the easiest ones for salespeople to reach, and the ones they most frequently do.

A good place to start our study of power and influence in the corporation is in the national political arena. When we speak of "corporate politics," we usually think we're using a metaphor that applies an image of our public, political sphere to the private world of the workplace. But turn the metaphor on its head for a moment. Consider the possibility that what goes on in Washington, D.C., is, in reality, little more than a magnified version of what goes on in the workplace.

Whatever one's political leanings, it's hard to escape the fact that political motivations and calculations—that is, efforts to build one's base of power—may supersede the greater national interest time after time in government. That's true whether the issue at hand involves a pork-barrel project, the trading of votes in order to pass or block a bill, or, on the darker side of politics, a character assassination designed to kill the career of a politician.

Even the use of military force is sometimes strongly suspected to be motivated by certain political considerations as much as by a sober assessment of the nation's security.

IT'S A TRUISM IN SELLING THAT THE CONTACTS WITH THE LEAST POWER ARE THE EASIEST ONES FOR SALESPEOPLE TO REACH.

That our government is driven by political forces is obvious because of its openness and its public nature. For these reasons it can be harder to separate the words "dirty" and "politics" in the public arena. Yet corporate America is driven by those same forces—it's just more subtle, understated, and usually cleaner, because public money isn't involved. In business, you don't hear the language of politics. Instead, political agendas are sanitized by carefully crafted business language.

TITLE IS NOT INFLUENCE, AND YOU CAN SAY THAT AGAIN!

In trying to learn how corporations work, we must understand the difference between influence and title. Many sales reps take too much comfort in knowing a customer's formal organizational structure and their contacts' titles. In essence, those sales reps believe that influence simply flows from title, and that knowing who holds what title is enough to understand how power and influence work in a customer organization. "Yo—I'm at the VP level! How much higher do you want me to go?"

But, as anyone who's worked in a company for more than a week knows, title and influence rarely form a tight, one-to-one correspondence. We need to view them independently.

Some people have both a high title and high influence. Most U.S. presidents would be in this group—but not, perhaps, a lame duck who has become wildly unpopular, or one who has lost influence as a consequence of a major scandal or some other form of political damage. In the corporate setting, the company president and other senior executives would seem to naturally fit into this same group. And while this is true in general, we've already seen why it's not safe to assume that in every case. Remember Jim, the former VP of operations at AlphaCard, who got a new title but less responsibility? Or the XYZ Ltd. president who was fired shortly after Frank had so successfully won him over?

> TITLE AND INFLUENCE RARELY FORM A TIGHT, ONE-TO-ONE CORRESPONDENCE. WE NEED TO VIEW THEM INDEPENDENTLY.

At the opposite extreme are low title/low influence people. In government, this group is made up of the vast majority of civil servants and low-level political appointees. In business, it's most of the rank-and-file employees.

More interesting are the other two quadrants. In the lower-right quadrant are people of high title but low influence. They carry titles that are bigger than their actual level of influence. In national politics, one obvious example has historically been the vice president of the United States. Any number of old political jokes testify to the fact that a vice president, while perhaps able to get the ear more quickly of the chief executive or of certain colleagues in the corridors of power, has a title way out of proportion to his actual level of influence. Put simply, while the vice president of the United States bears the second most powerful title on the planet, he is far from being the second most powerful person on the planet. The same thing happens in corporate America.

Finding such high title/low influence people in corporate America is more difficult. Titles do not automatically signal one's membership in such a category. But every company has people with titles far out of proportion to their actual level of influence. Consider Jim at AlphaCard once again. His new title, vice president of special projects, is certainly grand. His influence, as we've seen, is nil.

So it is with many executives today who have reached a plateau. Some keep their spacious corner suites and reserved parking spaces. Some even get invited to key meetings, although that's rare. But they no longer have as many people reporting to them, and they no longer take part in the truly important decisions in the company. If they had big budgets at one time, they've lost them.

The last group is the most interesting: those with high influence and low title. In national politics, one obvious example is the first lady. In administration after administration over the last several decades, the president's wife has proved to be one of the most powerful people in the

> EVERY COMPANY HAS PEOPLE WITH TITLES FAR OUT OF PROPORTION TO THEIR ACTUAL LEVEL OF INFLUENCE.

world. Yet no spouse is acknowledged anywhere in the U.S. Constitution—the nation's organizational chart, if you will.

Who are these high influence/low title people in corporate America? Their sphere of influence is not written on their business cards. Nor are there many obvious clues. When I ask groups of salespeople for examples of such people, I'm often told "executive assistants." Such isn't the case, however. An executive assistant's influence is limited to the ability to communicate your desire to meet with her boss; it certainly does not involve, for example, setting policy or strategy for the company.

The fact is, no particular title or function within an organization is by definition high influence/low title. We cannot easily identify these people. Bottom line: We can't determine actual levels of influence in a corporate organization without doing our homework! I'll show you how shortly.

For a further illustration of how complex it can be to sort out influence and title in corporate America, consider a vice president of purchasing. In most organizations, he or she is someone with a high title but little influence. The salesperson who assumes that a purchasing department is an important decision-making body in a buying decision may mistakenly place the purchasing VP in the high title/high influence group. On the other hand, as companies adopt strategic sourcing practices, the same title could actually carry tremendous influence.

Two industries—automotive and large retail—offer two prominent examples of business sectors in which the purchasing function, because it is so central to their operation, is actually strategic and not merely administrative. In these industries, the purchasing VP is often an influential player.

Sales reps face a further challenge beyond just sorting out who really has the power. In almost all organizations, the more influence a person wields, the more difficult that person becomes for a sales rep to reach. The converse is also true: the less influential a person, the easier to reach.

THE FACT IS, NO PARTICULAR TITLE OR FUNCTION WITHIN AN ORGANIZATION IS BY DEFINITION HIGH INFLUENCE/LOW TITLE. WE CANNOT EASILY IDENTIFY THESE PEOPLE.

It gets worse. A corporate person unable to exercise influence inside his or her own organization often attempts to satisfy that need by turning outside, to the salesperson waiting at the doorstep. This game usually takes the form of: "I'm the decision-maker here."

In almost every case, truly powerful people understate their influence over a buying decision; lightweights overstate it.

In short, most salespeople call on low-influence people in their customer organizations because those people are by far the most accessible. Yet few salespeople are willing to admit to themselves that they regularly call on someone at a company with such low influence. Indeed, as salespeople spend time with a customer contact, it is easy to let the rapport that develops cause them to subconsciously confer influence upon that contact.

It's a lesson that Mark learned the hard way. One day, Mark called me in excitement to report that Charlie, his main contact at one of his big customers, had recently been promoted from VP to president of the company, a large paper mill. On the surface, that certainly sounded like a promising development. But as I asked more questions about what had led up to Charlie's sudden ascent, I began to have my doubts. The president whom Charlie had been appointed to succeed had recently been fired by the company's board of directors. This predecessor had been the first president in a generation to be hired from an outside company.

By asking more questions, I also learned that shortly after the new president arrived, he had begun a program of wholesale change. After about a year, however, the board could no longer deal with the intensity of change. They fired him and promoted Charlie, who had been with the paper company for thirty years and had overseen every *non-strategic* function in the organization. He had been head of purchasing, human resources, safety, the environmental department, and facilities management. Never once had

> IN ALMOST EVERY CASE, TRULY POWERFUL PEOPLE UNDERSTATE THEIR INFLUENCE OVER A BUYING DECISION; LIGHTWEIGHTS OVERSTATE IT.

> INDEED, AS SALESPEOPLE SPEND TIME WITH A CUSTOMER CONTACT, IT IS EASY TO LET THE RAPPORT THAT DEVELOPS CAUSE THEM TO SUBCONSCIOUSLY CONFER INFLUENCE UPON THAT CONTACT.

Charlie been an operations manager with production under his control. Nor had Charlie ever been the head of the sales department for the paper mill, which is another strategic function.

Given Charlie's history, it was clear to me that the board had decided to take more direct control of the company. The board members had promoted Charlie to the president's office so they could pull every string.

It took Mark almost a year of seeing that the board, not Charlie, was calling the shots at the mill. Only then was he able to accept the reality that Charlie was really not as influential a player at the company as Mark had thought—title notwithstanding.

The Starting Point: Understanding the Three Sources of Influence

As difficult as it can be for sales professionals to look at their customer contacts with complete objectivity, they must do so if they want to accurately analyze the level of influence a contact really commands. The sales pro's task, quite simply, is to discover who has clout and who doesn't.

Answering this question can get muddied by the chicken-or-egg syndrome. What some consider a source of influence, others argue is a consequence of that person's influence. Still, one doesn't have to answer the question of which is cause and which is effect to make use of the general principles below. So with that clarification, here are three sources of influence.

1. **Influence by association.** The first source of influence is by association with powerful others. Clearly, people derive influence by virtue of their association with somebody else who is an established, high-influence person. The first lady is a prime example. Certainly, many first ladies have been intelligent and capable women in their own right. But in the end, their influence has derived principally from their relationships with their spouses, U.S. presidents.

So it is in the corporate setting: People gain influence in part merely by their association with others of established influence. Consider, for example, a new department head hand-picked for his job by the CEO. He has yet to prove himself on his own merits, but he enjoys significant influence beyond his rank by virtue of his association with the chief. That's why I always instruct salespeople who are mapping out the power structure in a targeted account to understand who was hired by whom and who was promoted by whom. The exercise is one of the most reliable ways to get a fast read on an individual's level of influence.

And it's so easy, too. If Lisa, from our earlier example, in trying to sell financial software to a key account, had only asked this simple question, she would not have been blindsided by the CIO, who wielded greater clout than the CFO—Lisa's contact—despite the CFO's being the CIO's boss.

2. **Influence from contributing value.** The second source of influence is value contribution. It should be obvious that if people bring value to their organizations, their level of influence rises (as long as they also master the subtle art of gaining visibility for that value contribution). As we get further into this chapter, I will show you the practical applications of this basic principle.

3. **Influence from specific expertise.** Association and value contribution are the two core sources of influence in companies. The third source of influence, specific expertise, is actually ad hoc influence, wielded by someone with a high degree of knowledge in a very specific area of the company's business—despite having fairly low overall corporate influence. Such a person might not, for instance, be involved in guiding company policy or strategy.

The classic example is a company's decision to make a significant technology purchase. At such a time, the

So it is in the corporate setting: People gain influence in part merely by their association with others of established influence.

company's resident computer whizzes—the folks privately labeled as "geeks" or "propeller heads"—suddenly find themselves thrust into powerful roles as part of the team evaluating the options and making the selection. But once the choice is made, they likely revert to their traditional, lower-influence roles.

Putting Organizational Savvy into Practice

A critical step in understanding how organizations really work is a very personal one. As a sales professional, you must decide that you *want* to understand how they work. Indeed, to become a Business Resource, you must cultivate a desire to engage the political structures of your customer firms. You must have, as they say, a stomach for politics. This doesn't mean, however, embroiling yourself in the negative side of your customers' politics. And if you know what you're doing, you won't.

Armed with the knowledge that we must view influence and title separately, and with the awareness of the three sources of influence just identified, you can start to put these concepts into practice. That means always wearing your political glasses: attending closely to the subtleties and nuances in your discussions with contacts and developing a good sense for the language of politics, as it is encoded and sanitized into business terms.

It also means cultivating your ability to ask good questions. Wouldn't it be nice if you could simply ask contacts how much influence they have and get a reliable answer? That's why you must learn to piece together the puzzle that is the political landscape of your customer's organization from the questions you ask—questions that often appear to the customer contact as innocuous, unrelated to identifying the power players.

Two Useful Tools and How to Use Them

Let me give you two tools to help you identify influence within a customer company.

> TO BECOME A BUSINESS RESOURCE, YOU MUST CULTIVATE A DESIRE TO ENGAGE THE POLITICAL STRUCTURES OF YOUR CUSTOMER FIRMS.

> WOULDN'T IT BE NICE IF YOU COULD SIMPLY ASK CONTACTS HOW MUCH INFLUENCE THEY HAVE AND GET A RELIABLE ANSWER?

The first tool is obvious: the customer's organizational chart. We've already stressed that the organizational chart isn't enough on its own to identify influence, and that some companies are even eliminating them. Nonetheless, the organizational chart is a good starting point to get the names of the players down on paper.

One tactical tip—don't ask your contact for a copy of the organizational chart. Ask instead for a "little help piecing together the structure"—and start drawing boxes on a sheet of paper.

The second tool is to get profiles of key players—ultimately the most important tool for helping to identify who has what level of influence.

Before you get started on your efforts to profile key players, consider a few related points. Certain departments within an organization are almost always noncore and nonstrategic and therefore have lower influence. Examples could include the safety, environmental, or human resources departments. Purchasing, too, is usually a lower-influence department, except, as we discussed earlier in this chapter, in companies that have adopted strategic sourcing initiatives.

However, such influence can vary with the type of business in which a company is engaged. For example, at a company whose core business is manufacturing, the vice president of manufacturing would almost always be more influential than the vice president of manufacturing at a company whose core business is, say, distribution.

Another example is the VP of safety who, in most companies, is in the high title/low influence group. But in a transportation company, the VP of safety may actually have power because safety is central to the success of the company's operation. Even here, though, it's iffy. Powerful people just don't like the "safety" tag. It's more likely that, even in a transportation company, true safety-related decisions will be made by operations executives, not safety executives.

ONE TACTICAL TIP— DON'T ASK YOUR CONTACT FOR A COPY OF THE ORGANIZATIONAL CHART. ASK INSTEAD FOR A "LITTLE HELP PIECING TOGETHER THE STRUCTURE"—AND START DRAWING BOXES ON A SHEET OF PAPER.

Before you start making the rounds of Knowledge Calls, put together your own best guess of the organizational chart of the company. As you meet with your contacts, casually enlist their help in filling in the blanks on the chart and ask the questions that will help you profile the key players.

The questions you ask and how you ask them depend upon the contact with whom you're meeting. For example, if you're having a discussion with a truly good coach—someone who'll tell you anything because he wants you and you alone to win—then almost any question that will help you understand who truly has power and who doesn't is fair game.

In such a discussion, however, it's important to avoid asking even your best supporter, "Who is the decision-maker?" In the end you'll have to figure out the answer to that question on your own, having sized up the customer's political structure. The truth is that many people don't know enough about how influence really works to figure out the subtleties that reveal who truly has power in their own company. So don't take too much on face value, even from a good coach. This is why I even advise against asking another very popular Vendor/Problem-Solver question: "Who else should I be talking to?" The response almost always directs you to a low-influence contact.

With someone who is merely a "neutral contact"—in contrast to a "coach"—you need to be less direct. And with a potential "gatekeeper," exercise even more caution as you pose your questions.

THE SEVEN TELLTALE SIGNS OF INFLUENCE

However you frame your questions and whomever you ask, here are seven things to look for when you're trying to spot influential people.

1. **They control the gold.** There's little question that a person's level of influence and access to budget dollars are closely linked. Find out whose departments are getting the gold.

2. **They get staff.** Budget dollars and people are the two most prized resources in a company. A person's influence almost always has a direct link with the number of people under his or her direct control.

3. **They are change agents.** Companies or departments change not because circumstances change but because some individual says, "We will change." When you're trying to find influential people, look for major changes in a company or a department, and find out who is initiating or driving those changes.

4. **They are hired or promoted by powerful people.** Since association with powerful others is a source of influence, it is a key piece of information for salespeople to learn in every sales campaign. Part of the task of profiling your customer organization is to understand how long people have been with the company or in a specific department. What are their career paths so far? Where did they come from prior to joining the company? Who hired and promoted them? Are they part of the new regime or the old guard? In short, with which powerful people, if any, are they associated? If you pay attention to only one of the seven telltale signs of influence, make it this one.

5. **They have a successful track record.** Figuring out who are truly the fast trackers in the organization is central to your analysis of who's powerful and who's not. You're trying to find out what a person's career path has been, who's won the promotions and other advancements and added responsibilities, who's had the plum projects, and who's been successful with them. If you pay attention to only two of these seven telltale signs, make this the second most important one.

6. **They have an appropriate personal style.** Powerful people don't all fit the same mold. Some are flashy, others understated; they run the gamut of personality

types and management styles. Some may even be a bit eccentric. But most share an overall tendency to act appropriately, avoiding gossip, whining, disproportionate personal discussion, and the like.

Take the case of Joe, a director of engineering at a client's customer company. I met Joe when I made a joint call with my client's sales rep. This rep had been calling on Joe for more than a year. One of the reasons for our meeting was to try to figure out if Joe was really the power player his title would seem to indicate. There had been some doubt in the salesperson's mind. During our visit, Joe made an off-the-cuff comment about his company's manufacturing department. "Without my engineering department, manufacturing wouldn't be anywhere near where they are today." At that point his voice took on the confiding tone of gossip.

Whether or not Joe's assessment was accurate—and it may well have been—one thing became immediately clear to me. The fact that he had made this comment to two outsiders, one of whom, me, he had never met before, was one compelling piece of evidence to take us off the fence: Joe was not a real mover and shaker within his company.

We weren't surprised by what happened next. Two months later, a major reorganization occurred, and Joe, who'd had seventy-five people reporting to him as director of engineering, was "promoted" to vice president of engineering services—with a staff of one.

7. **They've worked in or managed the most important departments or projects.** Remember Charlie's rise to president of the paper mill? He had worked in all but the most important departments. Pay close attention to career paths.

People who lack influence usually put up smoke screens to prove otherwise to you. Conversely, truly powerful people often put up smoke screens to make you think

PEOPLE WHO LACK INFLUENCE USUALLY PUT UP SMOKE SCREENS TO PROVE OTHERWISE TO YOU. CONVERSELY, TRULY POWERFUL PEOPLE OFTEN PUT UP SMOKE SCREENS TO MAKE YOU THINK THEY'RE NOT POWERFUL.

they're not powerful. That's why, if you intend to succeed in your own personal transformation to Business Resource, you must scrupulously seek to spot these seven telltale signs of influence in every sales situation.

SELLING REDEFINED: DECISION-MAKER REDEFINED

Consider the remark of former British prime minister Margaret Thatcher: "Being powerful is like being a lady. If you have to tell people you are, you aren't." The truly powerful don't talk about their power. They don't flaunt it. They don't need to. In reality, most go to some lengths to deny that they are powerful or are even involved in some important buying decisions.

By now you probably understand why I suggest you not use the term "decision-maker" and why I think a search for such individuals is a waste of time. As you begin to internalize the concepts of power and influence, it will become more clear to you why the term is so terribly misleading. Most so-called "decision-makers" have been granted their authority by a higher power. Hence, my preferred term for the person who nominally makes the decision is "designated decision-maker."

Only those salespeople who embrace an understanding of influence and politics in an organization will succeed in the new era of selling. To reach that goal, they must put aside attitudes of being "above politics." Instead, they must rise to the level of astute observers of—and indirect participants in—their customers' political structures.

Remember, your sales plan is only as strong as the contacts in the customer company that support it, and those strong contacts are getting harder to identify and reach.

BY NOW YOU PROBABLY UNDERSTAND WHY I SUGGEST YOU NOT USE THE TERM "DECISION-MAKER."

REMEMBER, YOUR SALES PLAN IS ONLY AS STRONG AS THE CONTACTS IN THE CUSTOMER COMPANY THAT SUPPORT IT.

chapter 5

"Sales reps will add value by their knowledge, or they will be replaced by technology-enabled selling. They must become more like consultants and business managers."

—Wendy Close, Gartner Group

UNDERSTANDING THE CUSTOMER'S BUSINESS

As I said, "Find the decision-maker" is the selling profession's most common cliché. There's a close second: "Know your customer's business."

This phrase has always been a mantra in even the most elementary seminar on improving sales skills. However, in spite of all the sales trainers and managers who exhort front-line salespeople to understand the customer's business—and despite all the sales professionals who say with smug confidence that they do—the most common complaint my firm hears from senior executives about salespeople is, "They don't understand my business."

If customer business knowledge was important in selling's old paradigm, in the new one it's a matter of survival. The words of Wendy Close above testify to that conclusion. Customers are infinitely better educated and more informed about what they want to buy, where they can buy it, how to use it, and even how much they should pay. They no longer need salespeople for any of these things. Since a customer has little need for salespeople as a source of information—their biggest value contribution in the past—salespeople must bring value in some other way.

THE MOST COMMON COMPLAINT MY FIRM HEARS FROM SENIOR EXECUTIVES ABOUT SALESPEOPLE IS, "THEY DON'T UNDERSTAND MY BUSINESS."

Indeed, they must create value for customers or face extinction.

The good news is that customers, especially customer executives, are increasingly inclined to buy from the supplier who demonstrates the greatest knowledge of that customer's business. Only then will the executive feel confident that the supplier has any hope of creating value for the company.

A survey conducted by *Sales & Marketing Management* magazine in 1998 concluded, "Customers are demanding salespeople with a deeper knowledge of their business, who can help them solve business problems. Salespeople who master those skills will be more in demand than ever. . . . [T]hose who don't? They might be headed for the unemployment line."

WHAT COLOR ARE YOUR GLASSES?

Why do salespeople fail to meet such a basic and widely understood standard as knowing the customer's business? Where's the disconnect?

It starts with how they see their value as salespeople. For example, the Vendor salespeople, whom I profiled in Chapter 2, see very little need to understand a customer's business. Many of them operate more like a human product catalog, rattling off features and benefits to the customer in the manner I described in Chapter 2: "Stop me when you hear something you like."

Admittedly, most Vendor salespeople aren't quite this overt with their product-focused mindset. Nonetheless, even the slicker Vendor salespeople see little real need to understand the customer's business, although they may sometimes give it lip service. "What for?" they think to themselves. "Once the customer sees a demo, it's all over but the cashing of my commission check."

But Vendor-level salespeople aren't the most serious problem. We know they care little about understanding the customer's business. Between salespeople's universal

CUSTOMERS, ESPECIALLY CUSTOMER EXECUTIVES, ARE INCREASINGLY INCLINED TO BUY FROM THE SUPPLIER WHO DEMONSTRATES THE GREATEST KNOWLEDGE OF THAT CUSTOMER'S BUSINESS.

awareness that they need to understand the customer's business and the executives' experience that salespeople fail to understand their business, there is a less obvious gap—which is therefore more insidious. The problem occurs not with Vendors but with salespeople who operate at the Problem-Solver level.

Problem-Solvers approach a customer or prospective customer with a thorough knowledge of their own products, their own solutions, their own company's abilities. They then attempt to identify the customer's business problems that their solutions can help solve.

It's not that this Problem-Solver approach is bad. It's just incomplete. Whatever you, as a Problem-Solver, sell, the majority of your selling efforts are most likely aimed at trying to find a customer pain that can be relieved with your solution. But as I say in Chapter 2, when all you sell is hammers, it's funny how everything can start looking like a nail. If you sell inventory control software, you go in search of inventory control problems, and so on.

On one level, of course, doing just that is a prerequisite to successful selling and bringing value to the customer. Certainly it's the salesperson's job to find a customer pain that the salesperson can ease.

However, that's also why most salespeople honestly believe that they *do* understand their customers' business. They do understand the business need that the customer has for their solution, but their understanding usually stops there. The Problem-Solver's knowledge of the customer's business is myopic, limited to a narrow set of business challenges that rarely extend to a truly holistic view of that customer's business.

Think of it this way: Do you view your selling situations through Vendor glasses? Problem-Solver glasses? Or Business Resource glasses? Most salespeople would like to believe that they view things through Business Resource glasses. But if your search for the customer's business problems focuses on challenges associated with the solutions you

MOST SALESPEOPLE HONESTLY BELIEVE THAT THEY *DO* UNDERSTAND THEIR CUSTOMERS' BUSINESS. THEY DO UNDERSTAND THE BUSINESS NEED THAT THE CUSTOMER HAS FOR THEIR SOLUTION, BUT THEIR UNDERSTANDING USUALLY STOPS THERE.

have to offer, you're not really viewing your customer's world as a Business Resource would.

As a Business Resource, it should be your goal to view the customer's business more from the vantage point of its CEO than from that of your day-to-day contacts.

LOOK FOR THE RELEVANCE

Shifting our perspective enables us to put our solution, and the business problems that it solves, into the much broader context of the customer company's *entire* business picture. Moreover, a Business Resource view of the customer's business is essential if we ever hope to create demand from our customers. And creating demand from customers can happen only if we create value for them—which, in turn, can happen only if we have a deep knowledge of their business.

There are no new concepts here. Yet acquiring knowledge of the customer's business is deceptively difficult for sales reps, not because the knowledge itself is complicated to acquire, but because many sales reps don't see the relevance of understanding the customer's business to the depth that selling at the Business Resource level demands. Once salespeople truly embrace the concept of becoming a Business Resource and recognize just how relevant gaining such depth of knowledge is, this step is one of the easier aspects to implement.

Consider the following situation. One client of mine, a provider of software to the financial services industry, had been trying to break into a large prospect in that industry. The software company's sales efforts were based on recognizing that its prospective customer had a well-defined, compelling business need for its solution. That business need was evident from the demands by the prospect's field sales force for remote access to that company's information about *their* customers. This information resided, of course, in the home office's computers. This business need could be filled—almost perfectly—by my client's software.

However, this particular business issue, while quite near to the hearts of the prospect company's sales team, was not even on the radar screen of the company's senior management. Thus, a proverbial no-brainer business fit between my client's solution and the prospect's "business need" continued to go unmet.

Gary, my client's sales representative, was stumped. Only after he stepped away from his overly narrow view of the prospect's business need did Gary succeed with this company. Here's what he did. He asked for a meeting with his contact, which he positioned as wanting to "leave his products at the door so as to go into homework mode in order to get a more complete picture of the prospect's business environment."

In the course of meeting with his contact, Gary identified four recurring themes about senior management's business priorities: (1) "accelerating the product launch cycle," (2) "implementing a territory management initiative" (this referred to an initiative to optimize the yield of its field salespeople), (3) "restructuring the company around market segments" (as contrasted with its current product-based structure), and (4) "expanding into the insurance industry."

Interestingly, Gary would be able to show that his software could make a contribution to only one of these four *senior management* business priorities, the territory management initiative. What's more, from a solution fit perspective, this particular fit wasn't nearly as strong as was the fit between Gary's software and the business need expressed by the prospect's sales force. But as you've just seen, the sales force's so-called "business need" didn't register with senior management.

Armed with this far more holistic awareness of his prospect's business, Gary, with his contact's support, next pursued a Business Presentation opportunity with senior management. In the course of that presentation, Gary subtly displayed his awareness of senior management's four

THIS PARTICULAR BUSINESS ISSUE, WHILE QUITE NEAR TO THE HEARTS OF THE PROSPECT COMPANY'S SALES TEAM, WAS NOT EVEN ON THE RADAR SCREEN OF THE COMPANY'S SENIOR MANAGEMENT.

business priorities. Then, before he discussed his solution, the prospect's senior vice president made two comments: "You've done your homework well," and "Your timing is very good—these are some of our key initiatives."

Gary received the nod that he was seeking, and he proceeded, with his contact, to implement a solution that addressed both the original business need identified by the sales force, the one that had not been even a blip on senior management's radar screen, and the territory management business need, a much smaller undertaking for my client. The moral of the story? Sure, you know you have to look for "hot buttons" (business needs)! *But make sure they're hot buttons to people of high influence.*

Ask yourself one question: Could you, like Gary, count on your prospects to buy from you based more on the depth of your understanding of their business than on the strength of your offering?

So, which glasses do you wear? How do you look at the value of gaining customer business knowledge?

- Through Vendor glasses: "How can I get this useless discussion about their business back to a discussion about my product?"

- Through Problem-Solver glasses: "How can I identify a business need for my solution?"

- Through Business Resource glasses: "How can I use my knowledge of the customer's business to establish credibility and make a value contribution to this company?"

CUSTOMER BUSINESS KNOWLEDGE: THE ULTIMATE COMPETITIVE WEAPON

Consider another situation. Nan is a strategic account salesperson for a major credit card transaction services company. Before making a presentation to the president of a large Chicago-based financial institution, Nan dedicated her selling efforts to learning about this prospective customer. She used the usual public sources, of course, but she also used something more important, which I explained in

Chapter 3: Knowledge Calls with low-to-mid-level contacts at the company.

When the time came for her presentation, Nan used the first few minutes to confirm her perception of four things: the customer's business profile, its key business drivers, its major initiatives and priorities, and the specific business issues driving the need for Nan's solution. She concluded her brief summation by asking the chief executive, "Let me do a quick reality check. Are we in the ballpark with our perceptions of your business?"

The CEO paused several seconds, then replied, "You have a better understanding of our business than many of the people who work here. I know your boss is here, so I shouldn't be asking this question right now, but are you interested in coming to work for us?"

Nan didn't go to work for the customer's firm. But the CEO's job offer to her didn't bode well for her competitors at this account.

On the surface, this scenario may not sound too different from what many salespeople do. But it is. That's because Nan didn't limit her discussion of the customer's business to only those business issues driving the need for her solution. She went much further, taking a holistic view of the customer's business. The difference may appear minor, but it's enormous, as both Gary and Nan learned. And it's what separates even the most business-oriented Problem-Solver from a true Business Resource.

GETTING STARTED: ATTITUDE IS EVERYTHING

Let's spend a few minutes on the drier details of how you actually gain your insights into the customer's business. As a starting point, keep in mind that knowledge of your customer's business is derived from two sources: publicly available information and information in your customer's head. The first is gained mostly from trade reference materials and various sources on the Internet, in particular, the company's own Web site. The second source is gained from Knowledge

> "LET ME DO A QUICK REALITY CHECK. ARE WE IN THE BALLPARK WITH OUR PERCEPTIONS OF YOUR BUSINESS?"
>
> THE CEO PAUSED SEVERAL SECONDS, THEN REPLIED, "YOU HAVE A BETTER UNDERSTANDING OF OUR BUSINESS THAN MANY OF THE PEOPLE WHO WORK HERE."

Calls with contacts at an account or prospective account during which you put aside discussions of your customer's needs and your solutions and strive to gain from your customer a strategic understanding of the big picture of that customer's business (See Chapter 3.). The remainder of this chapter and the next discuss how to use these two sources.

But before you even embark on the task, I want to emphasize this fact: *The how-to of customer business knowledge starts with attitude, mindset, and discipline.* It's not enough to pay lip service to the philosophy of leaving the product at the door—you have to live that philosophy at a much deeper level.

I WANT TO EMPHASIZE THIS FACT: *THE HOW-TO OF CUSTOMER BUSINESS KNOWLEDGE STARTS WITH ATTITUDE, MINDSET, AND DISCIPLINE.*

Suppose you follow up on a lead to a prospective customer, one that you're pretty sure is qualified and worth a meeting. When you phone your contact, she says, "Yes, we're interested in your software" (or whatever solution your company sells). "We're still in the very early stages of looking, but could you meet with me and give me a demo, and tell me more about it?"

Many salespeople would like to think they'd respond by *not* doing exactly what this prospect requested, but by attempting instead to gain more control of the sales situation. However, the practical reality is that most salespeople would do just as the prospect asked.

Except for the Business Resource. It shouldn't surprise you that the Business Resource would respond along these lines:

> Sure, I'd be happy to tell you more about our solution. In fact, if I might suggest a format for the meeting, our experience has been that the better we understand our customers' businesses, the more value we bring to those customers. With this in mind, let's get together, and I'll give you a quick snapshot of what our solutions can accomplish—a 30,000-foot overview—but I'd like to dedicate the bulk of our meeting to gaining a deeper understanding of what you're about as a company and what you're looking to accomplish. Make sense to you?

Notice that the Business Resource doesn't ignore the customer's desire to learn more about the product. That wouldn't be wise. He merely wrestles some control of the sales cycle and begins positioning himself as a Business Resource, not a demo-happy peddler.

CUSTOMER NEEDS SPRING FROM CUSTOMER BUSINESS ISSUES

Notice also that the Business Resource doesn't use the Vendor/Problem-Solver term, "understand your *needs*." To truly demonstrate that you are a Business Resource, you must convey a different message from that of only wanting to understand a prospect's needs. Try something along the following lines:

> "The better we understand your *business*, the more value we'll be able to bring to you."

Understanding the *business* versus understanding the *needs*—it's an important distinction, one that further distinguishes the Business Resource from the Problem-Solver, because the Business Resource knows that customer needs spring from customer business issues. Seeking to understand only a company's needs implicitly ties the conversation back to your solutions, a Vendor/Problem-Solver outcome.

Granted, in the course of your meeting you attempt to gain some understanding of the prospect's needs. However, as a Business Resource, you use this meeting primarily to start differentiating yourself as the one salesperson who truly wants to understand that company's business.

Customers have been getting smarter; they see through the smoke screens of salespeople who claim a desire to understand their business when all they're really doing is looking for a problem their solution can solve. From your earliest dealings with a prospective customer, and throughout all of your encounters, you should regularly check whether you are coming across as a true Business Resource—or just a hammer in search of a nail.

Even when a sales rep is sincerely attempting to understand a customer's business beyond that which relates only to the product she's selling, customers often don't get it. They've been "trained" in the ways of Vendor/Problem-Solver buying.

To be sure, customers don't necessarily make it easy for you to switch styles. For years, they've been programmed to limit their discussions with salespeople to only those things that relate directly to the sales rep's product and company. So even when a sales rep is sincerely attempting to understand a customer's business beyond that which relates only to the product she's selling, customers often don't get it. They've been "trained" in the ways of Vendor/Problem-Solver buying. A salesperson may ask a customer a question that applies very broadly to that customer's business, only to elicit an answer that applies very narrowly, and is relevant only to the customer's needs. The salesperson concludes, often erroneously, that the customer doesn't want to talk about his business, he wants to talk about his needs. The salesperson may be secretly elated; now the customer is talking within her comfort zone.

The sales professional should conclude instead that this customer just hasn't been trained yet in the ways of Business Resource buying.

Remember: You've arrived as a Business Resource when you leave your products at the door and when you've trained your customers to also leave your products at the door.

Who's in Charge Here?

When you take control of a sales situation, you turn a customer's request for information about your solution into a prime opportunity—an opportunity to position yourself as the Business Resource who first seeks a deep understanding of the customer's business. In that way, you are accomplishing something else as well. By subtly moving from asking the customer for the next step in the sales process to steering the process yourself, you have reached another Business Resource milestone.

Always remember that you know more about selling than customers do about buying. Even though customers are smarter today about the many options they have, if they ask you to come in to tell them about your product or to give a demonstration, their request seldom reflects a carefully-thought-out buying process. Rather, it reflects a lack of understanding of how they should go about acquiring your product or service. In most cases, "show us what you've got" is merely a default request on the customer's part. You need to have supreme confidence that you can bring value to customers by helping them understand how to buy your solution. You are, in essence, setting the ground rules for the buying process.

Earn the Right to Ask

You already know that before going to visit a customer or prospect you need to develop what business knowledge you can about the company. Once you've established that a particular prospective customer represents a qualified opportunity, your next step is to get as much information as you reasonably can about the prospect firm, even before your very first meeting.

Start with the obvious: the company's Web site. Usually, companies of any substance have more information on their sites than you could hope to digest. If it's a publicly held company, its annual report and other investor information is usually found on the site, too. If its Web site is inadequate, search a few of the countless other Internet-based repositories of company information.

Your preparation in learning everything you can about a company from these public information sources before meeting with any contacts not only gains you knowledge that is valuable in itself, but also earns you the right to dig deeper when you finally meet to conduct your Knowledge Calls.

A Basic Outline for Your Quest for Business Knowledge

Although I am providing you with a structure for understanding a company's business, there is no ready-made list of questions you should ask as you go about the process of doing so. Many salespeople might try to create such a list,

> IN MOST CASES, "SHOW US WHAT YOU'VE GOT" IS MERELY A DEFAULT REQUEST ON THE CUSTOMER'S PART. YOU NEED TO HAVE SUPREME CONFIDENCE THAT YOU CAN BRING VALUE TO CUSTOMERS BY HELPING THEM UNDERSTAND HOW TO BUY YOUR SOLUTION.

approaching the task of understanding the customer's business in an overly structured manner, as if conducting a survey. Although that method might work for gathering and organizing information from written sources before you talk with live sources, too much structure can get in your way during an actual Knowledge Call. You need to respond to what is being said to you in a fluid, dynamic, and very interactive and conversational way.

Having conducted over a thousand Knowledge Calls, I've found a basic outline for characterizing a company's business that seems to apply universally. It has four parts.

1. **Customer's business profile:** Past and present facts and figures and other general descriptions of the customer (the company, business unit, department, etc.). The business profile might include information about the company's:
   - history and evolution
   - size and growth rate
   - milestones/key events in its evolution
   - core competencies
   - markets and customers
   - competitors and market share
   - culture and business philosophy
   - bread-and-butter products

2. **Customer's key drivers:** Any factors, internal to the company or external, that in some significant way affect the customer (the company, business unit, department, and so on). Key drivers might include:
   - market conditions
   - industry conditions
   - customer trends
   - the Internet and other technology-related factors
   - competitor trends
   - unusual shareholder pressures
   - operational issues
   - financial conditions

- supply chain issues
- staffing/employment issues
- regulatory environment and issues

3. **Customer's initiatives and priorities:** The things the customer (the company, business unit, department, etc.) is doing, or attempting to achieve, in response to the key drivers. Initiatives and priorities might include:
   - goals and objectives
   - strategies
   - important projects
   - operational changes
   - organizational changes
   - products, including those being added, those being de-emphasized
   - markets, including those being added, those being de-emphasized
   - policy changes

4. **Business issues related to the fit for your company or solution:** This is familiar territory for people in sales. Clearly, many of the first three categories (business profile, key drivers, and initiatives and priorities) may relate, even if only obliquely, to the fit for your solution. Still, there remains a need to drill down with specific questions that help you characterize, both qualitatively and quantitatively, the value the customer is seeking from your company or its solution, and that help you identify value creation opportunities. Many of these are "pain-related" questions aimed at gauging both the real, objective pain the customer is experiencing as well as the customer's perception of how serious that pain is.

   Fit-related questions might include those tied to:
   - implications of *not* implementing your solution (how well is the status quo working?)
   - specific business problems your solution solves
   - how results will be measured

- compelling events or circumstances driving the need for your solution (remember the Y2K issue?— a textbook example of a "compelling event")
- timing issues
- the customer's ability to implement your solution
- specific technical criteria
- return on investment

PUTTING IT IN ACTION IN A KNOWLEDGE CALL

When you're meeting with a customer trying to use this outline, don't feel you have to follow the above four elements in order. Instead, allow yourself to bounce back and forth among them. Avoid making your customers feel they've been accosted in a shopping mall by a marketer with a script.

One other caution. It's a good idea to leave questions related to your solution for later in the call. Once you move to those questions, it's often hard, for both you and the customer, to step back to the broader, more strategic questions.

Knowing what to ask is the easy part. The hard part includes developing the ability to "frame" questions (not just ask them), to process your contact's response, and to ask a next question based on that response.

Consider a typical Knowledge Call. Let's say during the course of the call's warm-up phase, you ask the contact how long she's been working for the company (something you should always learn). A little later you might add something such as, "So, Allison, you said earlier you've been with the company for five years. I'll bet not much has changed, huh?"

I can predict with near certainty that Allison will roll her eyes as if to say, "You wouldn't believe how much has changed," and will proceed to describe the changes for you. Exactly the result you're seeking.

That almost universal reaction gives you an opening to casually ask many other questions, such as, "What's driving

IT'S A GOOD IDEA TO LEAVE QUESTIONS RELATED TO YOUR SOLUTION FOR LATER IN THE CALL. ONCE YOU MOVE TO THOSE QUESTIONS, IT'S OFTEN HARD, FOR BOTH YOU AND THE CUSTOMER, TO STEP BACK TO THE BROADER, MORE STRATEGIC QUESTIONS.

the changes?" "What's their status now?" "What's their effect on your department and you personally?" and so on. This line of questioning focuses on a key aspect of what we're trying to understand about the customer company: *change*. Understanding how a company is changing is an essential part of understanding its business.

For example, suppose you're conducting a Knowledge Call at a paper manufacturing company and the contact happens to mention plans to put a new machine on the company's flexible packaging line. That should trigger a whole series of questions: "What were some of the reasons behind the decision to install the new machine?" "When will it go into operation?" "Will it replace an existing machine, or will it add capacity or open up a new product line?" "Whose baby is the project?"

You must keep your strategic sense of curiosity well-tuned and ask the basic questions of "Who, What, Where, When, and Why." If you remain flexible, you can thoughtfully process the contact's responses, and your next question will flow more naturally. Understanding the customer's business is easier than you may think.

How Much Knowledge Is Enough?

None of this means you need to develop so deep an understanding of your customer's business that you could compete with an army of highly specialized consultants. Such consultants might be brought in by the customer's board to dissect the company on a microscopic level and make recommendations for a sweeping redirection of its strategic focus. That's not your job. It *is* your job to learn enough so that you can answer "Yes" to the following two questions:

1. Am I confident that I know significantly more about this customer's business than my competitors do?

2. Could I demonstrate, in a Business Presentation with this customer's senior management, an understanding of

AM I CONFIDENT THAT I KNOW SIGNIFICANTLY MORE ABOUT THIS CUSTOMER'S BUSINESS THAN MY COMPETITORS DO?

COULD I DEMONSTRATE, IN A BUSINESS PRESENTATION WITH THIS CUSTOMER'S SENIOR MANAGEMENT, AN UNDERSTANDING OF ITS BUSINESS THAT IS DEEP ENOUGH TO MOTIVATE MANAGEMENT TO BUY FROM ME ON THE STRENGTH OF THAT UNDERSTANDING?

its business that is deep enough to motivate management to buy from me on the strength of that understanding?

While it's naive to think customers will always buy from you on that basis alone, you should execute every sales campaign as if that were the case.

If you reach the depth of knowledge enabling you to answer yes to those two questions, you will possess an enormous competitive advantage. Your competitors are almost guaranteed to show, at best, a knowledge of the customer's business limited to only a few issues directly related to the need for their particular solution. In the name of "understanding the customer's business," your competitors will articulate what they understand to be the customer's problem—the customer's need—and show, in turn, how their solution addresses that need. They shall remain Vendor/Problem-Solvers, while you operate as a true Business Resource.

YOUR COMPETITORS ARE ALMOST GUARANTEED TO SHOW, AT BEST, A KNOWLEDGE OF THE CUSTOMER'S BUSINESS LIMITED TO ONLY A FEW ISSUES DIRECTLY RELATED TO THE NEED FOR THEIR PARTICULAR SOLUTION.

PICKING YOUR TARGETS

Who should be the target of your efforts to gain knowledge about the customer's business? The short answer is: almost everyone at the account. Your coach network—that group of contacts at the customer or prospect firm whose support you've already won—should be your primary source of customer knowledge. If they are true coaches, they are both willing and able to share with you what's happening inside the customer company. But your efforts don't stop with them.

Recall our discussion of the prospect who calls asking for a demonstration of your product? This contact is an ideal candidate for starting you off on the quest to gain business knowledge about the prospective customer.

Even gatekeepers can be terrific sources of business knowledge. These are the individuals, self-appointed and otherwise, who keep others in the company "safe" from salespeople. What's more, one of the best ways to disarm and soften a gatekeeper is to turn a discussion—the very topic of which might reinforce a gatekeeper's desire to block you—into a discussion of the customer's larger business issues. This tactic for disarming gatekeepers, by the way, is easily one of the best-kept secrets in selling.

You can't be afraid to ask challenging questions that make the contact think. In fact, doing so almost certainly increases your credibility with your contact. However, at the same time you must quickly identify the extent of the contact's *desire* to discuss various topics with you and his or her *ability* to do so. If, for example, you are asking a relatively low-level contact about the company's long-term strategic direction, only to find that the contact doesn't seem to know answers to any of your questions, you should downshift quickly to questions that relate only to the contact's more limited perspective. Although you want to ask business-oriented questions that challenge contacts, you want to make sure that your contacts are comfortable and feel useful in helping you gain insight about their company.

As you seek customer business knowledge, select whom to approach first and start with low-to-mid-level contacts. Don't try to gain your business knowledge from senior executives. Your goal is to possess business knowledge before you meet with the executives.

This lesson was learned the hard way by a sales rep I know. Steve works for a telecommunications supplier. After he heard my exhortations that salespeople need to understand the customer's business and also get to executives, he tried to put his new knowledge into action without paying enough attention to the subtleties of implementation. In his enthusiasm, Steve overlooked my point about having some business knowledge before meeting with an executive. Phoning a senior executive at one of his largest prospective customers, he managed to get the meeting, which on its own was a surprise. When he sat down with the executive, he asked a number of questions about the business. After about five minutes of this, the senior executive grew

ONE OF THE BEST WAYS TO DISARM AND SOFTEN A GATEKEEPER IS TO TURN A DISCUSSION—THE VERY TOPIC OF WHICH MIGHT REINFORCE A GATEKEEPER'S DESIRE TO BLOCK YOU—INTO A DISCUSSION OF THE CUSTOMER'S LARGER BUSINESS ISSUES.

DON'T TRY TO GAIN YOUR BUSINESS KNOWLEDGE FROM SENIOR EXECUTIVES. YOUR GOAL IS TO POSSESS BUSINESS KNOWLEDGE BEFORE YOU MEET WITH THE EXECUTIVES.

angry—and didn't hide it. "If you want to sell something to me," the executive said, "I expect you to understand my business *before* you come to see me."

While this exec's response may have been a bit extreme, it's not that far from the norm. Few top executives have the time to educate salespeople about their business. When you're planning a one-on-one meeting with an executive, learn everything you can before the meeting, and limit the number of questions you ask to a few high-level inquiries. Keep Steve's experience in mind.

GET MILEAGE FROM YOUR KNOWLEDGE

Finally comes the issue of using the base of knowledge you've acquired. Its primary function is to gain executive access and conduct Business Presentations, which I cover in Chapters 6 and 7, respectively. Whether or not you formally use the knowledge you've gained, such as in a Business Presentation, your very efforts to gain it enhance your status as a Business Resource in the eyes of the customer. That's your reason for being.

As this chapter's opening quotation says, "Sales reps will add value by their knowledge, or they will be replaced by technology-enabled selling."

IT'S ALL ABOUT UNDERSTANDING THE CUSTOMER'S BUSINESS. AND IF YOU'VE DONE YOUR HOMEWORK, YOUR MISSION AS A NEW ERA SALESPERSON—CREATING VALUE FOR THE CUSTOMER AND DEMAND FOR YOUR COMPANY—WILL NATURALLY FOLLOW.

Knowledge of what? Your product? Customers already have it. The customer's dog's birthday? He doesn't care. No, it's all about understanding the customer's business. And if you've done your homework, your mission as a new era salesperson—creating value for the customer and demand for your company—will naturally follow. You will be counted not only among the survivors in the redefined world of selling but also among the nouveau elite.

chapter 6

"Yes, Virginia, executives do want to see salespeople."

—Anonymous

HOW TO GET TO EXECUTIVES

One thing that will never change, new era of selling or old, is that the biggest decisions in any company will be made at, or require support from, the top of the organization. The most important commitments a company makes are decisions involving, for example, operating philosophy, policy, strategy, budgets, significant changes in employee count, major purchases, and key supplier relationships. Such decisions determine the very fate of the enterprise. The bigger the commitment, the higher it must travel up the ladder.

Although, as we discuss in Chapter 4, many traditional corporate hierarchies of the old era of selling are morphing into strange, new organizational structures perceived better suited to a new era of business, it's hard to imagine a time when there won't be some version of the "people at the top."

What's more, if you accept Andy Grove's claim that "salespeople are not going to be involved with order-taking and information flow at the most basic level," and if you also agree that their role is about creating value for the customer and demand for their own companies, which is a central theme of this book, then you probably require little convincing that executive access plays a vital role in the

ONE THING THAT WILL NEVER CHANGE, NEW ERA OF SELLING OR OLD, IS THAT THE BIGGEST DECISIONS IN ANY COMPANY WILL BE MADE AT, OR REQUIRE SUPPORT FROM, THE TOP OF THE ORGANIZATION.

new paradigm of selling. So I won't belabor the topic of the *need* to get to executives.

Yet the notion of calling on senior management has always met with resistance from salespeople—plenty of resistance. Have you heard any of these objections before? "We're already calling on the decision-makers." "We'll alienate our regular contacts." "Senior management couldn't care less about our products—and besides, executives don't see salespeople." "It's a rubber stamp at that level."

These spoken objections reflect one of two distinctly different realities:

1. salespeople who know that they should be calling at the executive level but don't know how to do so or what to do when they get there—which is, ultimately, a fear-driven reality;

2. salespeople who truly believe that all these objections apply to them—which is, ultimately, a Vendor-mindset-driven reality.

Neither of these *has* to be the reality for salespeople as we move into the new era of selling.

WHAT EXECUTIVES WANT TO SEE

The fact is, executives do want to see sales professionals—if those sales pros know why, when, and how to meet with them. Moreover, you won't alienate your contact if you've proven yourself to that contact as a credible Business Resource, not just a glad-handing Vendor who'll embarrass him in front of his boss.

It's certainly true that a bad meeting with a customer executive, unlike most other customer meetings, is worse than no meeting at all. And actually getting to senior management is harder than simply knowing that it's important to do so. But if you're committed to doing what's necessary to get out of your own comfort zone and to demonstrating to your customers' executives that you are truly a Business Resource who brings value and is therefore worthy of their

YOU WON'T ALIENATE YOUR CONTACT IF YOU'VE PROVEN YOURSELF TO THAT CONTACT AS A CREDIBLE BUSINESS RESOURCE, NOT JUST A GLAD-HANDING VENDOR WHO'LL EMBARRASS HIM IN FRONT OF HIS BOSS.

time, then—on the strength of that commitment alone—you're well on your way to success in the new paradigm of selling.

As you learn how to reach that level, aided by the information that follows, you will gain the confidence and the tools to get you to the highest levels in your customer organizations. Quite possibly you will find a level of professional satisfaction that you never thought possible when you were selling in the old era.

PURPOSE OF EXECUTIVE MEETING: ALIGNMENT, NOT DECISIONS

A prerequisite to learning how to get to executives is to first understand the *purpose* of the executive meeting. That's because its purpose—confirming alignment—is so radically different from the mainstream argument of "getting the decision made."

In the old paradigm of selling, getting to executives was considered important by most salespeople primarily for the purpose of having the executive "involved in a decision." Frankly, that erroneous basis for the executive meeting was the reason for so few successful outcomes. Involvement in the decision is becoming even less relevant in the new paradigm of selling, as executives delegate more and more day-to-day purchasing decisions to lower levels. Instead, the focus of executives, as far as supplier relationships are concerned, is becoming centered more on the strategic "fit" or "alignment" between their company and a supplier.

For years, my experience with clients has borne this out. I've consistently found that executive access efforts based on alignment are always more successful than those based on getting the executive "involved in the decision."

I present several examples of what I mean later in this chapter as we look at real-life executive access examples. What you'll see in all of those examples is a common theme: taking the purpose for the executive meeting out of the context of "getting to the decision-maker" and placing it where

IN THE OLD PARADIGM OF SELLING, GETTING TO EXECUTIVES WAS CONSIDERED IMPORTANT BY MOST SALESPEOPLE PRIMARILY FOR THE PURPOSE OF HAVING THE EXECUTIVE "INVOLVED IN A DECISION." FRANKLY, THAT ERRONEOUS BASIS FOR THE EXECUTIVE MEETING WAS THE REASON FOR SO FEW SUCCESSFUL OUTCOMES.

THE FOCUS OF EXECUTIVES, AS FAR AS SUPPLIER RELATIONSHIPS ARE CONCERNED, IS BECOMING CENTERED MORE ON THE STRATEGIC "FIT" OR "ALIGNMENT" BETWEEN THEIR COMPANY AND A SUPPLIER.

it belongs: in the context of "confirming alignment" between your company and the executive's company.

Once a salesperson internalizes the proper context for the executive meeting—confirming alignment—all other aspects of the process seem to fall into place. Correctly understanding the executive meeting's purpose also goes a long way toward breaking down the gatekeeper mindset, which so many contacts would otherwise invoke to block a salesperson who referred to "getting the executive involved in the decision."

> ONCE A SALESPERSON INTERNALIZES THE PROPER CONTEXT FOR THE EXECUTIVE MEETING— CONFIRMING ALIGNMENT— ALL OTHER ASPECTS OF THE PROCESS SEEM TO FALL INTO PLACE.

ESTABLISH MUTUAL COMMITMENT

Confirming alignment has two parts: establishing mutual commitment and verifying company-to-company compatibility. Let's tackle the commitment part first. Most executives place enormous value on commitment. That's why if you succeed at one thing in the executive meeting, it should be to credibly display your commitment to the executive's success. Credibility builds as a result of your energy, enthusiasm, and knowledge of the customer's business.

Interestingly, not all salespeople can pull off the "energy" and "enthusiasm" parts; it might not be in their nature to be high energy. Nevertheless, all salespeople can succeed at displaying commitment credibly if they're effective at demonstrating knowledge of the customer's business.

Take the case of Carl, an engineer by education who is a salesperson for a large chemical company client of mine. Carl is as low-key as they come. So his presentations don't have the electricity that is commonly associated with a "great" sales presentation. Yet he is among the most consistent performers in executive presentations that I have ever worked with. He's received more offers of employment from his customers' executives than any of my other clients' salespeople.

Why is Carl such a hit with executives—and his employer? How has he mastered credibility? You already know the answer: He is a master at demonstrating knowledge of the customer's business, the main ingredient in the "credibly displaying commitment" recipe.

Remember that in talking about commitment, I use the phrase "*mutual* commitment?" All salespeople recognize the need to show their commitment to the customer company. Even Vendor-level salespeople know this.

The Business Resource has an additional and equally important concern: clarifying the *customer's* commitment. The Business Resource knows that any commitment to a supplier company is most reliable when it emanates from an executive. The Business Resource is a nearly fanatical steward of his own company's resources. He parcels out these resources to prospects and customers in proportion to the reciprocal commitment—and he wants his customers to understand that. By the way, the Business Resource gains enormous respect from customers by doing this.

THE BUSINESS RESOURCE IS A NEARLY FANATICAL STEWARD OF HIS OWN COMPANY'S RESOURCES. HE PARCELS OUT THESE RESOURCES TO PROSPECTS AND CUSTOMERS IN PROPORTION TO THE RECIPROCAL COMMITMENT—AND HE WANTS HIS CUSTOMERS TO UNDERSTAND THAT.

VERIFY COMPANY-TO-COMPANY COMPATIBILITY

The second part of confirming alignment with customer executives is that of verifying company-to-company compatibility, which is sometimes known as the "philosophical fit." I discuss this again in Chapter 9.

When executives consider a supplier relationship, they are acutely aware of ensuring compatibility between the two companies in terms of values, strategic direction, technology orientation, core competencies, and the like. They look beyond the "product fit."

Janna is a strategic accounts salesperson for a financial software company. Her prospect was looking to replace all its financial software applications. In a very traditional buying cycle, Janna had made it to the short list, but her competitor, the dominant player in her company's traditional market space, was firmly in the lead going into the final presentation. The competition had her beat hands down on features and functionality, and it was clearly the number one choice of the prospect's CFO.

Janna knew from her Knowledge Calls that the CEO would be attending her presentation. Having done her Knowledge Calls well, she knew that this CEO was practically betting his company on "Webifying" it, as the CEO referred to it internally. Consequently, during the presentation she went to some lengths to discuss her own company's strategic direction of migrating the company's entire application to the Web, itself betting the farm on "Webifying" all its applications.

The only time the CEO made any comments during the presentation was when he asked Janna a few questions about her company's direction. Then he left the meeting. A few days later, much to the dismay of the CFO and bewilderment of her competitor, Janna received the good news. She had slain Goliath with a sling that was armed with philosophical fit, not with the ostensibly superior solution.

SHE HAD SLAIN GOLIATH WITH A SLING THAT WAS ARMED WITH PHILOSOPHICAL FIT, NOT WITH THE OSTENSIBLY SUPERIOR SOLUTION.

TIMING ISN'T EVERYTHING—BUT IT'S VERY IMPORTANT

Now that we've discussed the *purpose* of the executive meeting as confirming alignment versus getting a decision, we're ready to talk about how to *get* the meeting. The starting point is the timing of the meeting.

A recent article in a national business publication suggests that a salesperson should approach a customer executive only at one point in the sales cycle: early in the campaign, when, according to the article, executives are involved in setting the strategy for the purchase. Although it's true that salespeople should make their approach early rather than late in a typical campaign, this article paints too narrow a picture of the typical sales cycle. Its author is from the computer software industry, in which buying cycles tend to be highly structured; that is, a company decides it needs a particular kind of software, establishes a budget, and assigns a buying committee to select a vendor and/or software package. In those kinds of situations, the article's advice is accurate.

Across other industries, however, that buying paradigm is less common. Most sales campaigns are not the highly structured processes so typical of a software buying decision. There is a wide range of types of sales campaigns and situations that warrant a salesperson's calling on executives at many different times. Besides, in the redefined world of selling, a central role of the salesperson is creating demand, a role that has little to do with the "timing of a deal."

In considering when to approach executives, keep in mind that you must create opportunities, not just await them. While some openings to call on senior executives at a customer company arise on their own, most do not. So part of your job as a Business Resource is to create situations that offer a legitimate business reason for you to take the initiative in approaching a customer executive.

When to Stay Away

Let's first look at three key times *not* to attempt to approach executives.

1. **During the vendor selection process in a well-defined buying cycle.** This cycle is like the typical software sales cycle I just described. When the buying process is highly structured, senior executives usually confine their role to deciding early in the process the strategic objectives of the purchase and whether the company should make the purchase at all. They then delegate vendor selection to another individual or group. When a company is in the vendor selection stage and you ignore its structured buying process by attempting to go to senior management, you're likely to seriously damage yourself.

2. **After you've been told by a contact not to approach a senior executive.** You must hone your ability to sense gatekeepers so you can avoid using the kinds of words that prompt a contact to discourage you from going to senior management. Once a contact specifically tells

IN THE REDEFINED WORLD OF SELLING, A CENTRAL ROLE OF THE SALESPERSON IS CREATING DEMAND, A ROLE THAT HAS LITTLE TO DO WITH THE "TIMING OF A DEAL."

YOUR JOB AS A BUSINESS RESOURCE IS TO CREATE SITUATIONS THAT OFFER A LEGITIMATE BUSINESS REASON FOR YOU TO TAKE THE INITIATIVE IN APPROACHING A CUSTOMER EXECUTIVE.

you not to approach senior management, you are almost always better off honoring that demand. This is why I advise salespeople to purposely leave vague the "next step" discussion at the end of a Knowledge Call with a suspected gatekeeper. Don't give him the chance to tell you not to contact senior management.

If, however, you're absolutely sure that your contact lacks any real influence and can do you no harm if you ignore his demand, and if you are certain that yours is clearly the dominant solution and will be quickly recognized as such by the executive, then it's usually worth the risk.

Two caveats, though: Don't attempt to go around your contact unless you're certain of your ability to get the meeting—hell hath no fury like that of a gatekeeper scorned. And don't attempt it if the gatekeeper is in a position to sabotage the project once the sale is made. In most cases you are better off if you look for another situation, or create one, that would legitimize your going to senior management, and perhaps doing so via another contact.

3. **After losing a deal.** When someone makes a buying decision in favor of your competition, to go to that person's boss to get that decision reversed is inevitably a political lose-lose situation. Very few bosses second-guess a subordinate's decision, much less one who has been given specific authority to make that decision. You will permanently damage your relationship with that contact, with the executive, and probably with everyone else at the company.

There are exceptions here, too, however. The most prominent exception arises when you can credibly demonstrate that the buying decision will truly harm the prospective customer.

Consider the case of Robert, a salesperson who lost a huge deal to a competing firm. Robert knew that his

> DON'T ATTEMPT TO GO AROUND YOUR CONTACT UNLESS YOU'RE CERTAIN OF YOUR ABILITY TO GET THE MEETING—HELL HATH NO FURY LIKE THAT OF A GATEKEEPER SCORNED.

> VERY FEW BOSSES SECOND-GUESS A SUBORDINATE'S DECISION, MUCH LESS ONE WHO HAS BEEN GIVEN SPECIFIC AUTHORITY TO MAKE THAT DECISION.

competitor had recently dismantled the very department responsible for implementing the solution that the
customer had just agreed to purchase. It was easy for
Robert to prove that the competitor was incapable of
implementing the solution, a situation that posed a real
threat to the customer's business.

By raising the issue, Robert risked harming his relationship with his contacts if it appeared that his contacts
hadn't done their homework during the buying process. To
avoid that implication, he carefully framed his communication with the executive to take his contacts off the hook.
Robert's letter is shown on page 154 in the chapter on
pragmatic positioning. The senior executive reversed the
decision, took the business back from the competitor, and
gave it to Robert's company.

WHEN TO APPROACH EXECUTIVES

Once a sales professional starts to appreciate the visibility
that he can lend to his contacts by approaching executives
with a well-delivered message, executive meeting opportunities seem to multiply.

There are, of course, a few obvious times to approach
senior management, such as when an executive meeting is
built into a highly structured purchasing cycle. But other
opportunities to reach senior executives in target accounts
are as varied as the accounts themselves. If you are a sales
professional positioning yourself as a Business Resource to
the customer, you create those opportunities. Here are
eight good ones:

Opportunity 1: If you're entering a new account.
Although it's usually harder to get into a new account
by way of senior management, it's worth the challenge,
especially compared with the high likelihood of
encountering experienced gatekeepers at lower levels.
One of the biggest mistakes salespeople make when
calling on new accounts is to ask for the person who

ONCE A SALES
PROFESSIONAL STARTS TO
APPRECIATE THE VISIBILITY
THAT HE CAN LEND
TO HIS CONTACTS BY
APPROACHING EXECUTIVES
WITH A WELL-DELIVERED
MESSAGE, EXECUTIVE
MEETING OPPORTUNITIES
SEEM TO MULTIPLY.

handles the product or service that the salesperson sells. That guarantees being sucked into the gatekeeper vortex.

Opportunity 2: If you're inheriting an existing account. When an equipment supplier promoted Sarah to a strategic account assignment, she was given an account base made up largely of existing customers—accounts with huge growth potential. Sarah's first move was an instinctive one: to get on the phone to all the regular contacts whose names were in the files. It's a pretty safe bet that such contacts want to maintain the status quo, in which they control the relationships with suppliers.

Yet here was the chance for Sarah to make her first introduction to these customer companies by way of senior management without any great risk to relationships at lower levels. A salesperson in Sarah's situation always has one chance to contact a customer executive with impunity before approaching the traditional contacts. One of the oldest adages in selling that still applies is, "It's a lot easier to plead ignorance than to beg forgiveness."

But Sarah followed convention instead, phoned the regular contacts, and missed a huge opportunity to go higher up the chain of command.

Opportunity 3: If you have an existing customer and there's no active sales cycle. When there's no active sales campaign, an existing customer usually has its gatekeeping guard down. By suggesting to your contact that you'd like to "take the business relationship between our two companies to the next level" and that this would be an ideal time for a meeting with senior management, your request is likely to be met with high receptivity by your contact.

Opportunity 4: If something very good—or something very bad—has happened for an existing customer. When something particularly good has happened as a

WHEN THERE'S NO ACTIVE SALES CAMPAIGN, AN EXISTING CUSTOMER USUALLY HAS ITS GATEKEEPING GUARD DOWN.

result of something you, your company, or your solution accomplished, that's a wonderful time to go to senior management. They like to hear good news, and your day-to-day contact realizes that he's going to get some visibility as well.

When something bad has happened, you can score a lot of points and protect your contacts by going to senior management to face the music, apologize for the mistake, if that is in order, and show a clear plan to fix the problem.

Opportunity 5: If a buying decision has been made in your favor. When salespeople get the word from a contact that they've been awarded the business, most are too eager to take the order and run. But the Business Resource recognizes the value of having senior management be aware of and support the decision that's been made, because such support leads to a more successful implementation. At the same time, the gatekeeping instincts of your contact are usually lowered, and he's often more receptive to your meeting with the same senior executive whom he carefully guarded during the buying process.

Opportunity 6: If the designated decision-maker strongly supports your competition. It's particularly important to avoid discussing with this contact your intent to go to a higher level. When the designated decision-maker calls you on the carpet for going higher, you can plead ignorance. It's a risky proposition, but the alternative is almost certain defeat if this contact has enough muscle to gain a favorable decision for your competition.

Opportunity 7: If a prospect calls you. Suppose a low-to-mid-level contact representing a prospective customer calls to request a meeting about a specific solution. This scenario presents a potentially tricky situation. Most salespeople, in their excitement, assume they have a qualified prospect on their hands and eagerly share information about their solutions with the person who called them in. This unofficially designates that person as "their contact" at the account.

The Business Resource, however, is skilled in asking enough good questions to size up just how much ability this contact has to make a commitment. More than that, the Business Resource is able to articulate why it would help both the buyer and the seller to engage senior management sooner rather than later.

Remember: The purpose for your meeting with senior management isn't to get a decision made but to confirm alignment between your two companies. So she (the Business Resource) naturally meets with the contact who requested the meeting. But in the meeting, she starts to set the stage for an early executive meeting.

Opportunity 8: If you've been able to redefine what you're selling. The key here is to redefine the nominal product or service that the customer seeks in much broader terms that go well beyond the scope of your contact. This is an example of how the salesperson can create an opportunity. When you're selling something to be used only by the contact's department, it's difficult to justify going higher. But if you reframe your solution in terms that can speak to several departments in the buying company, your contact is less likely to be defensive about your going to other people, including to senior-level management.

> WHEN YOU'RE SELLING SOMETHING TO BE USED ONLY BY THE CONTACT'S DEPARTMENT, IT'S DIFFICULT TO JUSTIFY GOING HIGHER.

For instance, don't think of yourself as selling "supplies"—talk to your prospect about "supply chain management." In the same way, "trucking and shipping" becomes "logistics services," and "natural gas" becomes "an energy strategy."

This exercise—pragmatic positioning (it's the subject of Chapter 8)—is required for those whose ambition is to be seen as a Business Resource. Try it, and your path to the executive conference room is likely to be smoother.

WHICH EXECUTIVE TO APPROACH?

As you saw in Chapter 4, title and influence are seldom congruent. Thus, the most important criterion in deciding which executive to target is determining which executives at the customer company not only have an impressive title but also have the influence to accompany it. If you blindly sell to the so-called "C level" of the company (CFO, CIO, etc.) without verifying influence first, you are in for some major surprises and disappointments.

Another issue to consider is where you are in the sales cycle and with whom you have already made contact. Early in the cycle, when no contacts have been made, a salesperson can justifiably approach any executive in the company with little risk. But a sales rep who is heavily involved with a low-to-mid-level contact in the evaluation of a particular solution is often limited to calling on executives who are first "cleared" by the contact.

The target company's financial condition offers yet another factor in the choice of which executive to target. Fast-growing companies making a lot of money tend to push buying decisions farther down the ladder, while companies whose business is suffering tend to drive even the smallest spending decisions up to surprisingly high levels.

Consider also how new the concept is that you're attempting to sell to the target company. The more familiar the underlying concept you present, the less likely senior management is to take an interest in the buying decision. Therefore, it's very important for salespeople who want to consistently gain access to the highest levels to never let their overall message get stale, even if the product itself is. If you have an opportunity to communicate a message that "the world has changed"—in a legitimate, specific way, not merely by spewing a cliché—you're likely to get access further up the hierarchy.

Take a company that sells natural gas and electricity. These were once a company's most boring purchases, sold by public utilities at prices fixed by regulatory agencies.

> IF YOU BLINDLY SELL TO THE SO-CALLED "C LEVEL" OF THE COMPANY (CFO, CIO, ETC.) WITHOUT VERIFYING INFLUENCE FIRST, YOU ARE IN FOR SOME MAJOR SURPRISES AND DISAPPOINTMENTS.

When natural gas was deregulated in the late 1980s, energy salespeople had an opportunity to tell their customers how the world had changed because of deregulation. Today, deregulation is old hat, but energy salespeople have a new "world has changed" message: how the price of natural gas is increasingly determined by Wall Street speculators more than by traditional energy fundamentals such as weather. That redefined message offers a very credible basis for an executive meeting, focusing on a topic—energy—that at one time would never have been on the radar screen of senior management.

Finally, consider which executive initiated the current purchasing process, and which executive or executives are most likely to be affected in some way, for better or worse, by the purchase itself. Alternatively, look at which departments will be affected by the decision, and target the executive to whom all of those departments report, someone who is sort of a "highest common denominator." But never forget to confirm that the targeted high-title executive is also high in influence.

NEVER FORGET TO CONFIRM THAT THE TARGETED HIGH-TITLE EXECUTIVE IS ALSO HIGH IN INFLUENCE.

TWO DOORS TO THE EXECUTIVE SUITE

Bear in mind that I am talking about how to get to the *hard-to-reach* executives only. Clearly, if you're certain that you can pick up the phone and call an executive you know, and not only get the meeting but do so without alienating lower-level people, you should obviously do so— *if* the selling situation warrants an executive meeting.

Also, to emphatically reinforce themes I state earlier in this chapter, let the following two principles constantly guide your efforts.

1. **Always attempt to frame what you sell in the most strategic terms**. If you get stuck thinking, "Well, all I sell is widgets," then the executive will also view what you sell as "only widgets." As I point out earlier, if you view your own value proposition through "Vendor

glasses," you will be viewed through those same glasses by day-to-day contacts and executives alike. But if you see your value through "Business Resource glasses," that's how you will be seen.

2. **Stop looking for "the decision-maker."** Most sales reps focus too much on the question of who the decision-maker is and view the task of getting to senior management from that perspective. This is one of the biggest reasons that salespeople alienate contacts when they raise the notion of getting to senior management. Executives do more "approving recommendations" than "making decisions." So salespeople who communicate to their contact their desire to meet with senior management as a way to get to the decision-maker insult that contact.

Instead—and as a natural extension of what I discuss at length earlier in this chapter about confirming alignment—salespeople should view getting to senior management as a way of getting the high-level support needed that ultimately leads to successfully implementing the recommendation of the lower-level contact. Support, not decision—it's an important distinction.

It's unlikely that you'll reach an executive by using tactics touted as conventional wisdom, such as: treating the administrative assistant almost as if she were the executive (patronizing), calling during lunch (they've been on to this one for years), sending an attention-grabbing gift (tacky), or hand writing an envelope that looks like a personal note (deceptive).

In the real world there are only two practical ways for a salesperson to get to a hard-to-reach executive. One is to send a letter. The other is to go through a contact. These two methods apply in more than 90 percent of all situations.

If you take only one thing from this chapter, perhaps it should be this: Never put your executive access fate in the

> EXECUTIVES DO MORE "APPROVING RECOMMENDATIONS" THAN "MAKING DECISIONS."

> IN THE REAL WORLD THERE ARE ONLY TWO PRACTICAL WAYS FOR A SALESPERSON TO GET TO A HARD-TO-REACH EXECUTIVE. ONE IS TO SEND A LETTER. THE OTHER IS TO GO THROUGH A CONTACT.

TRYING TO WORK
THROUGH THE
EXECUTIVE'S ASSISTANT IS
THE MOST COMMONLY
USED ACCESS TACTIC, YET
IT'S WILDLY
UNSUCCESSFUL.

hands of an executive assistant. I emphasize this point because trying to work through the executive's assistant is the most commonly used access tactic, yet it's wildly unsuccessful.

But don't take my word for it; consider what executive assistants themselves have to say. When my firm launches a new engagement with a client, the client's executive assistants frequently attend the kick-off meeting. Without fail, they approach our consultants afterwards and thank them for educating salespeople on how to work the right way with members of their profession. Many relate stories of the endless types of patronizing manipulations salespeople attempt with them. Besides, as these assistants point out, "I don't decide who my boss meets with, he does—all I do is pass the request to him."

If you rely on an executive's assistant to grant you the desired access, you are likely to get diverted to someone else in the company whom the administrative assistant considers a more appropriate "sales" contact, and you'll wind up with no other way to gain access to that executive. The Business Resource doesn't rely on an administrative assistant to pick his or her contacts.

Even if an assistant does deliver your request for a meeting to the appropriate executive, your interests are not likely to be well served. No matter how meticulously you word your request, your message will probably be tacked on to the end of a long agenda of other items requiring the executive's attention and reduced to something like, "Oh, and some salesman from XYZ Company wants to meet with you to talk about software."

DOOR NUMBER 1: THE ACCESS LETTER

Conventional wisdom would conclude that a letter isn't much more effective than a telephone call in getting an executive's attention. Many salespeople might agree based on their own experience at trying to use letters.

The real problem isn't with the concept of a letter, but with the content and handling of the letters themselves. Most letters read like the work of a Vendor, not a Business Resource, triggering a near-automatic response from an executive of "sales letter"—if the letter even makes it past the assistant in the first place.

The two most common mistakes salespeople make in constructing letters to executives are (1) focusing too much on their own company and its solution, and (2) filling the letters with clichés, such as: "In today's fast-paced, competitive environment . . . ." As a result, letters consistently fall flat, leading to the conclusion by many in the profession that letters don't work.

By contrast, here are the five key characteristics of an effective access letter:

1. **The letter sells the *meeting*, not the solution.** Perhaps the most difficult leap for many salespeople to make is recognizing that the sole purpose of the letter is to get the meeting, not to sell the solution. Under most circumstances, an access letter should contain only one paragraph about the selling company and its value proposition. Of every word you write, ask yourself, "Will this word help me get the meeting, or is it something I should save for the meeting itself?"

2. **The letter displays knowledge of the customer's business.** Salespeople who operate in the Business Resource mode recognize that executives are more inclined to buy from them because of what they know about the customer's business than because of what the customer knows about them and their products. The executive access letter reflects this Business Resource mindset.

   It's really simple: The better your knowledge of the customer company, the more effective the letter. And your knowledge of the customer company turns on the quality of your sources. If you pull figures from the customer's Web site or from its annual report, for example, they are more sanitized and more generic than what you can get from an effective Knowledge Call on a lower-level individual in the target company.

A good Knowledge Call is always the best source. That source is not always available, however. That's when you need to get creative. Here's what Rachel, a sales rep for one of my clients, did when she visited a target customer, a large hospital. The Knowledge Call itself yielded only marginal information. The gold mine lay hidden in an employee newspaper Rachel found in the lobby. It contained a feature interview with the hospital's new chief information officer about his goals, strategies, and the like.

Because Rachel's company sold computer hardware, software, and services, a CIO would be an ideal executive for her to target. That the CIO was new meant he was almost certainly powerful—thus, exactly the person she needed to reach. Carefully drawing on the CIO's key goals and strategies from the article, but making no direct reference to it, Rachel crafted an access letter and won an appointment with the CIO.

3. **The letter displays a conversational, informal tone.** Write the way you speak—and keep in mind my college English professor's advice about simple language: "Don't utilize *utilize* when you can use *use*." Also use contractions, and don't be afraid to address the executive by first name. Indeed, when it comes time to presell the letter, a process we'll discuss in a moment, make sure to verify the correct spelling and preferred name or nickname.

4. **The letter is mechanically flawless.** When you're writing an executive access letter, don't type the final draft yourself. Give it to an experienced professional who knows grammar, spelling, punctuation, layout, and all

IF YOU PULL FIGURES FROM THE CUSTOMER'S WEB SITE OR FROM ITS ANNUAL REPORT, FOR EXAMPLE, THEY ARE MORE SANITIZED AND MORE GENERIC THAN WHAT YOU CAN GET FROM AN EFFECTIVE KNOWLEDGE CALL.

the subtle details of form and presentation for a business letter.

5. **The letter is presold to the executive's assistant.** The same assistant who might block or divert your telephone calls can prove very helpful in ensuring that your letter reaches the targeted executive. Before mailing the letter, call the assistant and explain that you'll be sending a letter to the executive, so you want to confirm spelling, title, address, and other such details. This conversation is itself an opportunity to alert the assistant that the letter is coming. The assistant is more likely to be helpful in guiding your correspondence to its intended recipient instead of tossing it in with the advertising brochures if you handle the discussion in a non-patronizing and non- "salesy" manner (for example, by not asking "How are you today?").

This preselling process is, on average, over 90 percent successful. If you find that assistants are frequently reverting to gatekeeper mode, you're probably handling some subtlety of the discussion incorrectly. Preselling is one of the most under-leveraged tactics in selling. Use it and you'll see what I mean.

EXAMPLES OF EXECUTIVE ACCESS LETTERS

The two examples that follow are actual executive access letters, which integrate all the points I recommend. Figure 6-1 is a letter that succeeded in gaining entry for my client, which was not at the time doing any business with the prospect, VISA. The salesperson, Paul Santini, was aiming to reach the right senior executive to create demand for his company's software solution. Paul's letter attempts to hook to the four business drivers and priorities known to be on the plate of the company's executive vice president. At first blush, the four bulleted items in the letter may seem nothing more than generic benefits of the value proposition of Paul's company, which appear in letter after

THE SAME ASSISTANT WHO MIGHT BLOCK OR DIVERT YOUR TELEPHONE CALLS CAN PROVE VERY HELPFUL IN ENSURING THAT YOUR LETTER REACHES THE TARGETED EXECUTIVE.

letter to targeted executives. On the contrary, they are among the top priorities and initiatives of its recipient, William L. Smith—and only William L. Smith.

Paul, the salesperson writing the letter, became aware of these priorities from Knowledge Calls he had conducted with lower-level contacts at VISA. Most of it came from the response that Paul's contact gave to a single question: "If I were a fly on the wall in one of Bill's staff meetings, what issues would I hear discussed as he went around the table asking his staff to report on what's happening?" (See Figure 6-1, page 111.)

LET'S DISSECT THE EXECUTIVE ACCESS LETTER

1. All information in the heading of the letter came directly from VISA. Paul made no guesses or assumptions about spelling, title, gender, or address. He remembered my telling him that, in my experience, more than 25 percent of all sales letters contain misspelled names.

2. The nickname in the salutation, Dear Bill, came from the executive's administrative assistant, who said, "Everyone calls him 'Bill.'"

3. The first two paragraphs demonstrate Paul's knowledge of Bill. This gets the recipient's attention without being showy or patronizing. Never make up this stuff!

4. Paragraph three followed by four bullet points are precisely the business issues Bill Smith is facing—not, as is typical in most sales letters, the four key benefits of the salesperson's product.

5. The next two paragraphs position Paul's request for a meeting.

6. Then three sentences—count 'em, three—position Paul's company and its value proposition.

7. The letter was "presold" to Bill's administrative assistant. Note that Paul is engaging the assistant, Marty

PARAGRAPH THREE FOLLOWED BY FOUR BULLET POINTS ARE PRECISELY THE BUSINESS ISSUES BILL SMITH IS FACING—NOT, AS IS TYPICAL IN MOST SALES LETTERS, THE FOUR KEY BENEFITS OF THE SALESPERSON'S PRODUCT.

1 → Mr. William L. Smith
Executive Vice President, Delivery Systems
VISA International
P.O. Box 8999
San Francisco, California 94128

2 → Dear Bill:

3 →   We recognize and respect the integral role that you and your staff have played in guiding VISA's service-driven image in the last ten or so years since your transition from IBM.

Certainly the introduction of the MIP project and the strategic implementation of computing systems to address VISA's fast-growing transaction volume are just two examples of where your presence is clearly felt.

4 →   Now, as VISA continues to strengthen its position as the premier payment system, and identify new and innovative transaction opportunities in market segments ranging from fast-food restaurants to insurance, you may be reviewing such basic delivery systems-related issues as:

- Ensuring continued network stability against a background of potentially explosive growth in volume from MasterCard and ACH transactions;
- Positioning VISA to quickly establish itself as the leader in debit card transaction processing (where system availability can be even more critical) in the event that the debit card concept gains wide consumer acceptance;
- Gaining enhanced marketing value from systems reliability to reinforce VISA's competitive position with card center managers and consumers; and
- Controlling the rate of growth of your network management staff while network growth itself continues.

5 →   Regarding these issues and others, Tricom Software can make substantial contributions that are consistent with your own delivery systems objectives.

That's why we're contacting you directly. Simply stated, we believe a mutual business opportunity currently exists. The benefits of this opportunity are directly related to the broad scope of your responsibilities.

6 →   As a point of reference, Tricom is the nation's largest privately held software systems company, with over twenty years of consistent growth. We are best known for our data and network management tools as well as application-specific products. We are also a broad-based systems support resource to other information-driven enterprises.

It is for these reasons that we request the opportunity to meet with you to make a concise business presentation on the above issues. (Perhaps Scott Curran and Rosland Smith would also be appropriate attendees.)

The purpose of this meeting is not that of a product presentation. Instead, its content is directed at our long-term business relationship, particularly as it relates to the delivery systems issues that you are facing.

7 →   Bill, we're eager for this opportunity for a brief meeting with you. I'll call Ms. Marty Davis in a few days to determine your availability for a 30-to-45-minute meeting.

We look forward to meeting you.

Cordially,

Paul Santini
PS:dr

Fig. 6-1

SAMPLE LETTER: HOOKING TO AN EXECUTIVE'S SPECIFIC PRIORITIES

Davis, in the right way, as a conduit to facilitate his request, not as a so-called gatekeeper who has the power to grant or deny him access to the chief.

Try this approach with some of your own sales situations (after your own Knowledge Calls, of course), presell it correctly, and you just might surprise yourself.

To further dispel the myth that letters aren't a good executive access tool, let's look at Figure 6-2, page 113. Here is a letter that attempts, at least to some degree, to hook to the executive's priorities. However, its core positioning is that of building on an existing relationship between the two companies.

Note the use of first names, especially that of "Happy." When Catherine Jones, the salesperson, presold this letter, she was told by the president's administrative assistant, "Everyone calls him Happy. In fact," the AA added, "half the people who work here don't even know his name is Edward."

Note further that only a single paragraph is dedicated to positioning the selling company and its value proposition.

Door Number 2: Work through a Contact

The second way for a salesperson to get to a hard-to-reach executive is through a contact. No sales dialogue better tests a salesperson's mettle than talking with a lower-level contact about getting to that contact's senior management. Such a conversation requires every ounce of confidence, business sense, and relationship skill you possess, along with a deep sense of the subtleties of the spoken word.

Mark Twain said that "The difference between the right word and the almost-right word is the difference between the lightning and the lightning bug." Frame your request well, and you just might become immune to competition at the account. Make a mistake, and you could alienate one of your best supporters—or perhaps create a gatekeeper for life.

NO SALES DIALOGUE BETTER TESTS A SALESPERSON'S METTLE THAN TALKING WITH A LOWER-LEVEL CONTACT ABOUT GETTING TO THAT CONTACT'S SENIOR MANAGEMENT.

Mr. Edward M. Paulus
President
Peachtree Chemical Company
2727 River Road, Suite 1700
Atlanta, GA 30339

Dear Happy:

For more than ten years now Peachtree and JBM & Associates, Inc., have enjoyed a mutually beneficial business relationship, primarily in support of the OSHA and DOT compliance efforts of your three Texas-based ethylene plants and Peachtree's internal transportation and logistics operations.

However, based on the changing profiles of both Peachtree and JBM, we believe an opportunity exists for an expanded relationship between our two companies. That's why I'm writing to you directly to request a brief meeting.

Specifically, as Peachtree continues to turn the corner from the last two challenging years, and with the leadership role you assumed last fall, Peachtree may be looking for ways to extend the capacity of its internal safety resources, especially in light of PT&L's skyrocketing growth and the surging demand for ethylene. JBM is uniquely qualified to support this objective.

JBM has changed, too. We've grown to become a $200 million company with more than 1,400 employees dedicated exclusively to the DOT, OSHA, and EPA challenges facing our customers. We accomplish our mission through a full range of safety/regulatory products and services.

The purpose of this meeting is not simply that of a JBM product presentation. Instead, its aim is toward setting a new direction for our business relationship in a way that supports Peachtree's sharpened focus on profitability.

With this in mind, I'll contact Ms. Tracey Cahill in the next few days with the hope of scheduling a 45-minute meeting with you.

I look forward to meeting you, Happy.

Cordially,

Catherine L. Jones

Fig. 6-2

SAMPLE LETTER: BUILDING ON AN EXISTING RELATIONSHIP

I give you some sample dialogues later in this chapter. The wording of those samples, like all executive access dialogues, is highly dependent on several factors. Here are the three most important:

1. **Personal relationships.** Surprisingly, a positive, long-standing relationship with a contact can actually be a hindrance. The contact frequently feels insulted by your desire to meet with a higher-up. Having believed all along that he has been able to make these decisions, he suddenly hears you saying you need to go to the boss instead. You must factor this perception into how you word your suggestion of an executive meeting. How warmly your contact responds to your suggestion of such a meeting offers a measure of whether the contact perceives you as a Vendor or a Business Resource. Remember, your contact's name is on that meeting.

THE NOTION IN SELLING THAT ONE CAN WORK HIS WAY UP THE CHAIN IN THE TARGET COMPANY OR THAT A CONTACT, WITH THE RIGHT CONVINCING, CAN INTRODUCE A SALESPERSON DIRECTLY TO EXECUTIVES TWO, THREE, OR MORE LEVELS HIGHER THAN THE CONTACT'S FLIES IN THE FACE OF REALITY.

2. **Intervening layers of management.** The notion in selling that one can work his way up the chain in the target company or that a contact, with the right convincing, can introduce a salesperson directly to executives two, three, or more levels higher than the contact's flies in the face of reality. More often, those at each level in the organization devise reasons why the buck ought to stop with them rather than go to higher levels. Anyone who's worked for more than a week in a corporate setting understands the political dynamics of going over the head of one's own boss.

That's why it's one thing to suggest a meeting with your contact and her immediate boss and quite another to suggest a meeting two or more layers above her.

If the executive you want to reach is your contact's direct superior, ask your contact to schedule a meeting and invite her boss. When you're going more than one level above your contact's boss, however, float a trial balloon with your contact on the relative merits of the meeting, indicating that you intend to seek a meeting with the executive.

But don't ask your contact's permission, don't ask if she thinks it's necessary, and don't ask her to arrange it. Instead, let the contact know your rationale for meeting with the executive and explain that you'll handle the request on your own, as you usually do in such situations.

3. **Your contact's influence.** Most executives meet with salespeople when requested to do so by almost any subordinate. However, a salesperson referred by a subordinate whom the target executive regards highly walks into the executive's suite presold. Although that same executive might agree to meet with a salesperson referred by another subordinate whom the executive views unfavorably, under those circumstances the salesperson goes into the executive suite carrying some serious baggage.

You don't always have the luxury of choosing the contact who will introduce you to the executive. Often, you must work through the nominal contact in the buying process or your own day-to-day contact. Still, as a politically savvy sales professional, you should know whether this contact is a heavyweight or a lightweight, and let that knowledge guide your decision either to work directly through the contact or to approach the executive yourself.

WORDS! WORDS! WORDS!

The one variable that trumps all others when it comes to getting to executives through a contact is how you word your request. The *numero uno* mistake is to ask some version of "Do you think we need to get [executive's name] involved in the decision?" Such a request is almost certain to annoy your contact, who probably believes that he or she, not the higher-up, makes the decision. It's also almost

A SALESPERSON REFERRED BY A SUBORDINATE WHOM THE TARGET EXECUTIVE REGARDS HIGHLY WALKS INTO THE EXECUTIVE'S SUITE PRESOLD.

THE ONE VARIABLE THAT TRUMPS ALL OTHERS WHEN IT COMES TO GETTING TO EXECUTIVES THROUGH A CONTACT IS HOW YOU WORD YOUR REQUEST. THE *NUMERO UNO* MISTAKE IS TO ASK SOME VERSION OF "DO YOU THINK WE NEED TO GET [EXECUTIVE'S NAME] INVOLVED IN THE DECISION?"

certain to elicit this response: "[Executive's name] doesn't get involved in these kinds of decisions."

As a Business Resource, you don't ask your contact's permission, and you don't ask if your contact thinks you need to meet with an executive. Instead, you propose with confidence that now is an appropriate time to discuss with senior management the direction in which you and your contact, or your two companies, are going together.

Carefully plan your entire discussion with the contact. It pays to practice your wording with your manager or with sales colleagues whose judgment you respect.

THE KEY OBJECTIVE ISN'T SO MUCH TO GET YOUR CONTACT ENTHUSED ABOUT THE DESIRED MEETING, ALTHOUGH THAT'S ALWAYS NICE, OF COURSE, BUT TO AVOID A SITUATION IN WHICH YOUR CONTACT FLATLY SAYS "NO."

The key objective isn't so much to get your contact enthused about the desired meeting, although that's always nice, of course, but to avoid a situation in which your contact flatly says "No."

WHAT "NO" REALLY MEANS

When a contact does naysay your suggestion of an executive meeting, you can interpret the refusal in one of four ways:

1. "I'm threatened by your meeting with senior management because I'm either going to look bad or my job security will be threatened."

2. "I don't want you to know that I don't have enough pull to get the meeting you're looking for. If I attempt to get the meeting and I'm unsuccessful, I've just demonstrated to you my lack of influence in my company."

3. "I don't think you [the salesperson] are executive credible, and my name is going to be on that meeting." This is a very common motive—one that's not voiced by contacts but is real nonetheless. Everybody wants to look good; if your contact thinks he or she is going to look good in the course of arranging a meeting between you and the executive, you will get the meeting. That is one more reason to continue working hard on your own executive credibility.

4. "I don't understand what's different now that requires senior management to meet with you that didn't require senior management to meet with you before." This is a clear indication that you've not positioned your request well.

Once the contact actually says "no," that almost always shuts the door—soundly. Therefore, you need to thoroughly analyze the potential for that outcome. If there's a realistic chance your suggestion of a meeting with senior management will result in a rejection by your contact, planning will help you anticipate the problem and prevent that "no" from ever being uttered.

CONTACT DIALOGUE IN ACTION

Let's consider how you'd approach a contact to win access to an executive in each of three quite different sales situations.

Situation #1: A buying cycle with a prospect who is definitely going to make a purchase. Since we're assuming that the dialogue takes place early in the cycle—where it should take place—you might say something like this as you speak to the contact:

> Our experience with companies similar in size and business philosophy to yours has been that executives don't want to get involved in exploring options and picking vendors. But they are very interested in assuring compatibility of philosophy and strategy between themselves and any supplier. My company has a similar interest in that corporate compatibility because we don't fit everywhere. Confirming this compatibility also makes it easier for us to continue investing our resources in proving the fit that we believe exists between our two companies.
>
> I wouldn't expect you to arrange the meeting; we're prepared to handle that ourselves. But I would like to confirm something with you. Our sense is that the final decision that you and the rest of the team make for this purchase will need to be blessed by [executive's name].

Would you agree with that assessment?

(Customer responds in the affirmative.)

Then we'll most likely direct our request to [him or her].

Situation #2: An existing contact at an existing customer with the purpose of expanding your position with this customer. Here you're dealing with someone who likely has a strong attachment to the status quo. You have to come up with some compelling reason why, suddenly, it makes sense for you to meet with senior management. "What am I, chopped liver?" your contact may think, or even ask you, if not in so many words.

In that situation, a good dialogue runs along these lines:

> Over the six years our two companies have worked together, your company has grown and changed and ours has, too. (Here it's a good idea to cite an example or two of those changes.) That's why we believe this is a great time to look at taking the business relationship between our two companies to the next level.
>
> I'd like to suggest a strategic, company-to-company meeting to explore the long-term direction of our business relationship. And if ever there were a meeting with our company that [executive's first name] ought to attend, this would be that meeting. Because its purpose isn't about day-to-day buying decisions but, rather, about setting a new direction in our business relationship. We want to show alignment between our company's direction and philosophies and yours. Make sense to you?

YOUR CONTACT WILL HAVE PLENTY OF OPPORTUNITY TO BASK IN THE GLORY OF HER ASSOCIATION WITH YOU WHEN THE MEETING ULTIMATELY TAKES PLACE.

Most likely, you've chosen your contact well and she agrees with your rationale for the meeting. The next step is to talk about how to arrange the meeting. In most cases, it's still a good idea to steer toward your sending a letter to the executive. This allows you to control the positioning. Don't worry; your contact will have plenty of opportunity to bask in the glory of her association with you when the meeting ultimately takes place.

In all of this you're attempting to create a message that the worlds in which your two companies operate have changed. You've taken the basis for an executive meeting out of the context of wanting to get the executive "involved in a buying decision" and put it into the context of a "totally new, expanded direction in your mutual business relationship"—a context in which it makes sense to engage senior management.

Situation #3: You're calling on a new prospect to begin the demand-creation process. The key to framing your request for an executive meeting with a new prospect is to describe to the contact what your company does in terms far broader than those within the purview of that contact. This is the time to use your most strategic terminology and to avoid "salesy" words and clichés.

Suppose your company is a large provider of office supplies and furniture to major corporations. Pretty mundane stuff on the surface. On the one hand, you could describe yourself to your contact this way: "We sell pens, pencils, and office furniture." With that description, the value proposition you offer is viewed as a commodity, to be referred to the prospect's purchasing department. On the other hand, you could say something along these lines:

> We sell nonproduction supplies. But the critically important thing to know about what we sell is that studies have demonstrated that every time a company spends $100 on non-production supplies, it spends an additional $150 in procuring those supplies. So the real issue isn't what supplies cost but what procurement model best aligns with the supply chain philosophy of your company. Our experience with companies similar in size to your own is that senior management is keenly interested in this business issue.

YOU'VE TAKEN THE BASIS FOR AN EXECUTIVE MEETING OUT OF THE CONTEXT OF WANTING TO GET THE EXECUTIVE "INVOLVED IN A BUYING DECISION" AND PUT IT INTO THE CONTEXT OF A "TOTALLY NEW, EXPANDED DIRECTION IN YOUR MUTUAL BUSINESS RELATIONSHIP."

IT'S ESSENTIAL THAT YOU CONVEY TO THE LOWER-LEVEL CONTACT THE FACT THAT YOU "SPEAK THE LANGUAGE" OF SENIOR MANAGEMENT.

It's essential that you convey to the lower-level contact the fact that you "speak the language" of senior management. And while that dialogue applies to one group of products—office supplies—some derivative of that message can usually be crafted for almost any kind of value proposition that a sales professional offers.

ARRANGE THE MEETING

Finally comes the task of setting up the meeting itself. If the contact is the one to attempt scheduling the meeting with the executive, it's a smart idea to give that contact the words, because he's not likely to do a good job of framing the request himself. However, it must not appear that you're spoon-feeding him. One of the better ways is to send a follow-up letter (most likely an e-mail) to your contact immediately after the discussion in which he agreed to arrange the executive meeting. The letter, of course, contains all of your positioning sound bites. The contact is likely to attach it to an internal memo, use it to extract the key words to communicate your request on his own, or—if it's an e-mail—forward the e-mail to the executive with a brief note of support of his own.

BECAUSE THE ERRONEOUS MAINSTREAM VIEW ON THIS POINT IS SO PERVASIVE, IT BEARS REPEATING: IT'S EXTREMELY DIFFICULT FOR A CONTACT TO GET YOU A MEETING WITH AN EXECUTIVE WHO IS ORGANIZATIONALLY ABOVE HIS OR HER IMMEDIATE BOSS.

If you're trying to get a meeting with just the contact and his boss, it's fine to have the contact schedule it. But if there are layers between your contact and the targeted executive, you're almost always better off trying to maintain control of the access process yourself. Because the erroneous mainstream view on this point is so pervasive, it bears repeating: It's extremely difficult for a contact to get you a meeting with an executive who is organizationally above his or her immediate boss.

YES, VIRGINIA, EXECUTIVES DO WANT TO SEE SALESPEOPLE

The fundamental redefinition of "selling" notwithstanding—or more accurately, because of it—getting to executives must become standard fare for sales professionals. As a starting point, you need to hold two convictions: a belief in the value that you, as a Business Resource, can create for those executives and can deliver to them, and a belief in the meeting's purpose as "confirming alignment," not "getting a decision."

Once you hold those convictions, continue to develop your executive credibility, measure every single word in your request, and you're there! And yes, they *do* want to see you.

chapter 7

Says the dog, lying on the couch in his therapist's office: "And then one day it occurred to me . . . what would I do with that car if I did catch it?"

—*The Wall Street Journal*, "Pepper and Salt" cartoon, created by Wildt

THE BUSINESS PRESENTATION

Like an introspective dog that chases cars, salespeople often wonder, "What would I do if I did get the executive meeting?"

LIKE AN INTROSPECTIVE DOG THAT CHASES CARS, SALESPEOPLE OFTEN WONDER, "WHAT WOULD I DO IF I DID GET THE EXECUTIVE MEETING?"

In Chapter 6, I exhorted you to leave your comfort zone and pursue more executive meetings. After all, what's the worst that can happen? If you think the answer is, "The executive says 'No' "—you're wrong! It's a trick question. The right answer is, "You get the meeting!" Let me explain.

A bad meeting with senior management is worse than no meeting at all. This is a meeting at which you cannot afford to drop a bomb. Remember Steve, the sales rep for a telecommunications supplier, who was thrown out of an executive's office for trying to conduct a basic Knowledge Call?

Kiersten, a sales rep for another client of mine, met with a customer executive only to have that session bomb as badly as Steve's. Kiersten walked the exec through a PowerPoint presentation on her laptop. Though her presentation nicely described her value proposition and her company, the executive quickly lost interest in her pitch.

THE TWO MOST COMMON MISTAKES THAT SALESPEOPLE MAKE WHEN MEETING WITH EXECUTIVES: EITHER THEY ASK QUESTIONS ABOUT THE EXECUTIVE'S BUSINESS—ESPECIALLY VERY BASIC QUESTIONS—OR THEY FOCUS ON THEIR OWN COMPANIES AND THEIR OWN SOLUTIONS.

Steve's and Kiersten's experiences illustrate the two most common mistakes that salespeople make when meeting with executives: Either they ask questions about the executive's business—especially very basic questions—or they focus on their own companies and their own solutions.

In contrast to Steve's and Kiersten's experiences, recall Nan's success only five minutes into her executive presentation to the CEO. When she asked the CEO if she was in the ballpark with her perceptions of the CEO's business, he offered her a job. Nan had not even started to discuss her solution or company. As I describe in Chapter 5, she had spent the first few minutes of the presentation simply—and quickly—confirming her understanding of the customer's key business drivers, major initiatives, and priorities.

Nan's presentation illustrates something that appears, on the surface, to be a minor point. After all, we're talking about merely five minutes of a one-hour meeting. Besides, the CEO already knows his own business. Tell that to Nan, who landed the account that eventually put a cool six-figure payout into her pocket.

The reality is that the difference between Nan's Business Presentation and Kiersten's solution presentation is like the difference between a diamond and good cubic zirconia—you have to look pretty closely before you see any differences, but the actual differences are immense.

In this chapter, I tell you about the Business Presentation—the most effective way to prove yourself a Business Resource when you get to a customer executive. Here, I attempt to establish the rationale behind the Business Presentation and why it is an irreplaceable tool for salespeople in the new era of selling. But the essence of my message is tactical, very "how-to," and it seeks to provide you with the details of developing and delivering one specific presentation format—the very same format that Nan used so successfully, as have the sales forces of hundreds of other clients.

This isn't to say the format I outline here is the *only* effective executive presentation format. However, once you master this one, you are able to discern if it is the ideal format for your specific situation, or if, out of an infinite number of isotopes of this format, any others are more effective.

I do not address the executive *dialogue*. Salespeople who become effective at executive-level *presentations* virtually always develop the ability to handle a wide range of one-on-one executive dialogue situations. In fact, it's my experience that to become good at executive dialogues, a salesperson must first become good at the Business Presentation with executives. It's sort of a rite of passage.

The most prominent trademark of the Business Resource is a single-minded focus on high-impact sales activities— those activities that yield dramatic results and that significantly shorten sales cycles. Of these, one stands out as the highest of the high: the Business Presentation. No other single event in a sales cycle has the impact of the Business Presentation. Yet, incredibly, they occur about as often as a traveling call in the NBA. Why? Salespeople have done all right without them. Until recently, a killer demo or compelling product pitch had been enough to cinch the deal.

Today, however, in the redefined world of selling, most of the face-to-face activities that made salespeople successful, e.g., the demo and its many variations, are on a slippery slope toward irrelevance, because customers today view demos as not being of sufficient value to conduct face-to-face when they can be done so much more efficiently via the Web.

Once optional, the Business Presentation is now integral to selling. Indeed, no salesperson can claim to be at the Business Resource level of selling unless the Business Presentation is a regular part of his or her sales repertoire.

WHY A PRESENTATION BEATS A DISCUSSION

One of the great ironies in the selling profession is that many salespeople are reluctant to conduct stand-up presentations. One assumes that salespeople would embrace every

IN FACT, IT'S MY EXPERIENCE THAT TO BECOME GOOD AT EXECUTIVE DIALOGUES, A SALESPERSON MUST FIRST BECOME GOOD AT THE BUSINESS PRESENTATION WITH EXECUTIVES. IT'S SORT OF A RITE OF PASSAGE.

opportunity to conduct presentations, but statistics, and my own empirical observations, prove that assumption wrong. This is one of selling's dirty little secrets. Consistently, most salespeople shy away from conducting presentations, or else they refer to a discussion they've had with a customer as a "presentation" because they "presented" their solution.

Frankly, salespeople aren't exempt from what surveys say is at the top of most people's fear list: speaking before an audience. And it is easy to see how that fear could be intensified when the audience is an executive in a key customer company.

Yet the value of the presentation in a sales campaign is immeasurable. It is more than a forum for communicating information to a large number of people. If the aim were merely to convey information, an e-mail would be cheaper and more efficient. But imagine a presidential debate occurring in a chat room, or reading John F. Kennedy's "Ask not what your country can do for you" in a letter to the editor. The great words of history and politics lose their punch when stripped of oral expression.

So do the great words of business.

An October 22, 1996, article in *The Wall Street Journal* reporting on a presentation to Wall Street analysts provides a graphic illustration:

> IBM will report its earnings today, but its stock, and possibly the broader market, could be more influenced by a presentation by IBM's CFO than by the numbers themselves. . . . What seems to matter most to analysts and investors isn't the official IBM earnings figures but rather the words and body language of Mr. _____.

The point? Presentations have an intangible power that far exceeds the simple trotting out of facts, figures, or information.

The world-class Business Resource recognizes all the concentrated power of presentations and uses it to his or her advantage. The presentation is a powerful vehicle for delivering your value message to customers and prospects.

FRANKLY, SALESPEOPLE AREN'T EXEMPT FROM WHAT SURVEYS SAY IS AT THE TOP OF MOST PEOPLE'S FEAR LIST: SPEAKING BEFORE AN AUDIENCE. AND IT IS EASY TO SEE HOW THAT FEAR COULD BE INTENSIFIED WHEN THE AUDIENCE IS AN EXECUTIVE IN A KEY CUSTOMER COMPANY.

THE POINT? PRESENTATIONS HAVE AN INTANGIBLE POWER THAT FAR EXCEEDS THE SIMPLE TROTTING OUT OF FACTS, FIGURES, OR INFORMATION.

PROPOSALS ARE CONFIRMATION TOOLS, NOT SALES TOOLS

Proposals are one of selling's most sacred cows; few other tasks are treated with more reverence. Yet your prospects seldom put a fraction of the sweat into reading your proposals as you do in writing them. Of the wide range of activities that can exist in the sales process, a customer's reading of a proposal is among the least likely to have an impact. That's true whether the prospect is a homeowner reading a proposal on replacement gutters or a corporate executive reading one on a potential consulting engagement.

Am I advocating that you eliminate proposals from your repertoire? Not at all. Instead, I want you to understand their true role. View the proposal as a *confirmation* tool, not a sales tool. Both you and your prospective customer should view the proposal primarily as a statement confirming the discussions and agreements you've already reached via your earlier calls and particularly your Business Presentation. After all, do you really want your entire selling effort reduced to the prospect's reading of your proposal and comparing it to those of your competitors?

Let's say you sell gutters to homeowners. The prospect calls, you scope out the job, ask some questions about color preferences and the like, shake hands, smile, and say, "Thanks, I'll mail you a proposal."

Or say you sell sophisticated technology solutions or management consulting. You spend several visits doing needs analyses, then hunker down with your staff to hammer out a proposal, which you hand deliver to the prospect. Then you start the follow-up process. "How are we looking?" "Can I answer any questions?"

Does either sales cycle sound familiar? Both reveal missed opportunities. If you were the gutter salesperson, you should have asked the homeowner for five or ten minutes at the kitchen table, then conducted a brief, informal presentation, perhaps with a few props to sell your ability to do the job better than anyone else. And if you were selling sophisticated technology or consulting services to a corporate

> AFTER ALL, DO YOU REALLY WANT YOUR ENTIRE SELLING EFFORT REDUCED TO THE PROSPECT'S READING OF YOUR PROPOSAL AND COMPARING IT TO THOSE OF YOUR COMPETITORS?

prospect, you should have arranged for a Business Presentation to the prospect's senior management, thereby selling your ability to do the job better than anyone else and ensuring management's support for the project's success.

In both cases your proposal should follow the presentation as a confirmation. What carries the sale are the strategy, words, and emotions of your presentation.

ROLE OF THE BUSINESS PRESENTATION IN A SALES CAMPAIGN

Many types of presentations might be done in a typical sales campaign. If they're done well, they are almost always a useful step in the sales process; a good demo, for example, can be quite useful under the right circumstances. Here I focus on one type of sales presentation in particular: the Business Presentation, aimed usually at an executive level in the customer/prospect organization.

In the previous chapter's discussion on getting to executives, I pointed out that the central purpose for getting to executives is that of "confirming alignment," not "getting a decision." In that vein, the purpose of a Business Presentation with a prospective customer is to establish the basis of the relationship that would exist between the two companies, not to get the deal closed, even though it strongly supports that end. Similarly, if the Business Presentation is with an existing customer, its purpose is to confirm the direction, or in some cases, set a new direction, for the business relationship between the customer company and the selling company.

Once salespeople grasp this notion, most of the other aspects of the Business Presentation follow logically. For those salespeople who can't get beyond "solution presentation," the Business Presentation concept never really grabs hold.

WHEN TO DO A BUSINESS PRESENTATION

A Business Presentation can be appropriate in many different sales situations. To name just a few, it can be the final

THE PURPOSE OF A BUSINESS PRESENTATION WITH A PROSPECTIVE CUSTOMER IS TO ESTABLISH THE BASIS OF THE RELATIONSHIP THAT WOULD EXIST BETWEEN THE TWO COMPANIES, NOT TO GET THE DEAL CLOSED, EVEN THOUGH IT STRONGLY SUPPORTS THAT END.

step in a highly structured buying cycle where you've made the shortlist; it can be an attempt to take a business relationship with a long-standing customer to a new level; it can occur in an early meeting with a prospective customer where you believe an opportunity exists to create demand; and it can take place in conjunction with a proposal presentation. You shouldn't have any trouble finding or creating presentation opportunities. Creating such opportunities is the stuff of Business Resource selling.

Since the purpose of a Business Presentation with a new prospect is that of establishing the basis of the business relationship, it should take place as early as practical in such a sales cycle. Establishing the basis of that business relationship benefits both the selling company and the buying company. It's within the context of the Business Presentation that the "fit" between the two companies is best communicated, allowing both companies to get an early sense of each other's commitment.

For similar reasons, the question of when to conduct a Business Presentation with an existing customer has a simple answer: "As soon as practical." If a salesperson has not already conducted a Business Presentation with his or her important current customers, it should be done. Few better ways exist for injecting freshness into a stale relationship or taking a good relationship and making it great, solidifying the commitment of the customer's senior management—which is not bad insurance against the bumps in the road that inevitably appear in any business relationship.

It's the responsibility of the salesperson to clearly articulate real business reasons for such a meeting. For example, changes are always taking place in the customer company, in your company, and in the general business landscape (take, for example, the Internet). Given these changes, the basis of the business relationship between the two companies must also evolve in order to support the development of future opportunities. This reality provides ample business rationale for a meeting with the executive

IT'S WITHIN THE CONTEXT OF THE BUSINESS PRESENTATION THAT THE "FIT" BETWEEN THE TWO COMPANIES IS BEST COMMUNICATED, ALLOWING BOTH COMPANIES TO GET AN EARLY SENSE OF EACH OTHER'S COMMITMENT.

of an existing customer, even one you've done business with for a while.

Hasn't the customer's world changed since the inception of the business relationship? Hasn't yours?

Who Should Attend the Business Presentation

The person, or people, that you most need in your Business Presentation are almost always the hardest ones to get to attend. Executives with real power are more difficult for salespeople to reach than are nonexecutives or executives without much power. So it's your job as a Business Resource to size up the account objectively and ask yourself the question, "Which executives' support is essential for the long-term success of the business relationship between my company and this customer/prospect?" Those are the senior management people you need to have attend your presentation.

It's also a good idea to include those individuals in the customer organization who are important to implementing the relationship day by day. The presentation meeting is an opportunity to give everybody in the account a chance to embrace the relationship with you and your company.

From your company, the attendees should include at least one member of your senior management team. However, it's critical to define the role that this executive from the selling company plays. In the old era of selling, the selling company's executive was at the meeting to "speak executive language" with the customer executive. It became, in effect, a meeting of the two executives, with the salesperson relegated to the job of chauffeuring his or her boss. Vendor/Problem-Solvers are comfortable passing off to their own executives the responsibility for the success of such meetings. The Business Resource does not let that happen.

The Business Resource recognizes that his or her own executive is at the meeting merely to voice support for and reinforce the commitments that the sales rep is making to the business relationship with the customer company. This

IN THE OLD ERA OF SELLING, THE SELLING COMPANY'S EXECUTIVE WAS AT THE MEETING TO "SPEAK EXECUTIVE LANGUAGE" WITH THE CUSTOMER EXECUTIVE.

is a critical point to remember: The sales rep's senior executive is at the meeting to voice support for what the sales rep says, not to run the meeting. In a sense, the executive subordinates his or her own agenda to that of the salesperson.

This exchange of roles can be uncomfortable, both for salespeople and for their executives. But salespeople have to learn to step up to that level of responsibility, and executives have to learn to check their egos at the door. When this is handled correctly, customers quickly come to realize that if they really want something done, they call the salesperson—the Business Resource—not the executive.

MANAGE THE MEETING, DON'T GIVE A SPEECH

Another key to a successful Business Presentation meeting is to remember that you are there to manage a meeting, not to give a speech. In a typical Business Presentation meeting, the presentation itself is anywhere from fifteen to twenty-five minutes long, yet the meeting as a whole lasts anywhere from forty-five minutes to two hours. One hour is the most common length.

Do the math, and you'll see that for more than half of the time the salesperson isn't presenting at all but is orchestrating the follow-up discussion. If the salesperson's attention during the meeting is too narrowly focused on the presentation itself, as is often the case, the result can impede effective management of the meeting. Sales managers must keep this same point in mind as they work with their salespeople to prepare each Business Presentation, reinforcing the salesperson's responsibility to manage every second of the meeting.

I hear a number of salespeople say, "My customers are more laid-back and informal. They'd be turned off by a formal presentation." Note that "formal presentation" is two words. A good stand-up Business Presentation to an executive should never have a stiff formality to it. It's far more effective with an informal tone to it, even though a tone of informality is actually harder to achieve.

THE SALES REP'S SENIOR EXECUTIVE IS AT THE MEETING TO VOICE SUPPORT FOR WHAT THE SALES REP SAYS, NOT TO RUN THE MEETING.

Content of a Business Presentation

Figure 7-1 (see pages 134–135) gives you a sample Business Presentation in outline form, modified from an actual presentation delivered by a technology company, which we'll call BMI, to a New York brokerage house, which we'll call John J. Renard & Company.

The presentation has a four-part structure:

Part 1. Confirming the selling company's understanding of the customer's business issues and business direction. This may be the most important component of a Business Presentation. Pages 4 to 7 of the sample show that component. Although this confirmation consumes only two to five minutes of the presentation, it's a critical step in establishing the salesperson as a Business Resource. Remember, the most common complaint executives make about salespeople is, "They don't understand my business." Recall Nan's success when she confirmed her understanding of her prospect company's key drivers, business initiatives, and priorities? There's no question that she won the deal solely on the strength of her knowledge of the customer's business.

If you do only one thing in a Business Presentation, it should be to establish that you understand the executive's business. Your goal is not to educate customers about their own business but to get credibility points for your understanding of their world.

Part 2. Positioning your own company and value proposition. This is your opportunity to show your stuff. The sample does this on pages 8 to 10. One might think this would be the easiest part of the presentation for a salesperson. Surprisingly, though, most salespeople find it difficult to develop an effective, succinct description of their own company and to position it in a way that goes beyond simply stating the facts. Yet do it you must, because this is your best opportunity to define in the mind of the customer how you want your company and value proposition to be viewed. This part of the presentation might take anywhere from five to fifteen minutes.

Part 3. Articulating the business fit. This is the salesperson's attempt to summarize the basis of the business relationship between the two companies. In the sample, this part is represented by a single page, page 11. It could range from just one central point up to about four points. The more homework a salesperson does on the target account, the easier it is to develop this business fit component of the presentation. If you closely review the entire sample presentation, you'll see that the content of the business fit on page 11 is derived from the content on pages 4 to 7 that demonstrates knowledge of the customer's business.

Part 4. Recommending a path forward. If you can't develop a recommended next step as the closing point of your Business Presentation, don't make the presentation. Every sales interaction must advance the sales cycle. It's your job to steer the customer to an appropriate next step in the sales cycle that will move the business relationship forward.

> EVERY SALES INTERACTION MUST ADVANCE THE SALES CYCLE.

It's remarkable how many customer presentations are made by salespeople with no specific recommendations for a next step. They prefer to leave that work up to the customer, even asking the customer outright, "What would you like us to do next?" Recognize that even though customers are smarter today about product options and pricing, most customers still don't know much about the process of buying, and they know even less about selling. That's your area of expertise. They're counting on you to recommend the next step.

So be a Business Resource and take ownership of that important part of the Business Presentation. Steer the sales campaign.

> SO BE A BUSINESS RESOURCE AND TAKE OWNERSHIP OF THAT IMPORTANT PART OF THE BUSINESS PRESENTATION. STEER THE SALES CAMPAIGN.

BMI was very clear in what it viewed as the most appropriate next steps in its presentation to Renard.

A Business Presentation
To:

John J. Renard & Co.

Investment Securities

Presented By:
BMI Corporation

Page 1

Presentation Objectives

- **Confirm BMI's Perception of John J. Renard's Business Direction and I/T Issues**

- **Establish BMI as a Resource and Technology Partner**

- **Identify a Path Forward**

Page 2

Agenda

- **John J. Renard & Co.:**
  - Profile
  - Key Drivers
  - Initiatives and Priorities
  - I/T Issues and Challenges
- **BMI:**
  - Our Strategic Shift
  - Our Securities Industry Commitment
  - A Business Partner
- **The Renard/BMI Business Fit**
- **Action Steps/Timetable**

Page 3

Renard: Profile

- **Founded in 1944**
- **Strong Capital Base**
- **Regional Player**
- **Businesses:**
  - OTC Stocks
  - Corporate Finance
  - Trading
  - Research
  - IPOs
- **Niche: Middle Market**
  - Emerging Growth
  - IPOs
- **1:1 Ratio/15% Growth**

Page 4

Renard: Key Drivers

- **The Internet**
- **Intensifying Competition**
  - Large Brokerage Houses
  - Discount Brokers
  - Banks
  - No-Load Mutual Funds
  - Brokerless Trades
  - Insurance Companies
- **Pressure on Margins**
- **Cyclical Market**
- **Fewer IPOs**

Page 5

Renard: Initiatives And Priorities

- **Effect a Paradigm Shift:**
  - Commission—>Fee-Based
  - Trader—>Financial Planner
- **Leverage Technology:**
  - Timely Information
  - Higher Volumes
- *Diversify:*
  - Wealthvest
- *Expand Product Portfolio:*
  - Fixed Income
  - Financial Planning
- *Focus on Core Competencies*
- *Maintain 1:1 Ratio/15% Growth*

Page 6

Fig. 7-1

SAMPLE BUSINESS PRESENTATION (PAGES 1–6)

**_Renard: I/T Issues
And Challenges_**

- **Develop and Implement a
  Business-Driven Technology Plan**

Page 7

**_BMI:
Our Strategic Shift_**

From   _To_

- **PCs**   • **I/T-Driven**
- **Servers**   **Business**
- **Mainframes**   **Solutions**
- **Software**
- **Peripherals**
- **Services**
- **E-business**
  Services

Page 8

**_BMI: Commitment to
Securities Industry_**

- **30+ Years Industry Involvement**
- **Full-Time Industry Staff**
- **Strategic Partnerships:**
  - ALP
  - Quotevest
  - XLI
  - Clearing House
    Resources, Inc.
- **Integrated Business Solutions**

Page 9

**_BMI:
A Business Partner_**

- **Client-Focused:**
  - Understanding Business
    Requirements
  - Understanding Financial Issues
- **Broad Base of Resources:**
  - Hardware/Software
  - Systems Integration
  - Web/E-business Expertise
  - Application Development
  - Business Partners
- **Partnerships with Strategic
  Customers**

Page 10

**_Renard/BMI:
Business Fit_**

- **Supports Renard's Commitment to
  1:1 Ratio and 15% Growth**
- **Accelerates Renard's Paradigm
  Shift**
- **Consistent with Renard's Core
  Competency Focus**

Page 11

**_Action Steps
Timetable_**

- **Conduct Phase I Study:**
  - Document Needs
  - Define Specific I/T Requirements
  - Develop I/T Strategic Plan
- **Present I/T Strategic Plan to
  Renard and Discuss Phase II
  Options**
- **Implement the Plan**

Page 12

Fig. 7-1

SAMPLE BUSINESS PRESENTATION (PAGES 7–12)

Incidentally, BMI's delivery of its presentation took about thirty minutes, which included a ten-minute case study overview in which BMI demonstrated how it had approached a similar challenge for another financial services company. With discussion, the entire meeting lasted about ninety minutes.

A Quick Word about Media

Keeping in mind that your presentation is not merely to deliver information to an audience, don't be too quick to automatically employ the default medium of choice in the business community: PowerPoint, or any other similar laptop-based presentation format. While such applications are wonderful for many other types of presentations, computer-based media tend to convey an image of product pitch, information dump, or "sales" presentation.

Sure, you can customize your presentation over an Egg McMuffin two hours before the meeting. Unfortunately, customers are all too aware of that. Computer-based presentations are often sterile and don't contribute to the level of intimacy that a world-class salesperson is attempting to create in a Business Presentation. Besides, it seems these days that anyone can create a whiz-bang PowerPoint presentation. That's why I advise against trying to prove you're a technologically "with-it" company via your use of PowerPoint.

I ADVISE AGAINST TRYING TO PROVE YOU'RE A TECHNOLOGICALLY "WITH-IT" COMPANY VIA YOUR USE OF POWERPOINT.

Having discouraged PowerPoint as a medium for Business Presentations, I do recognize that its use is unavoidable, even practical, in many situations. It certainly can get the job done. And it's cheap. However, a more effective medium for an in-person Business Presentation is the flip chart. Surprised? Most salespeople are. This "low-tech" medium offers many advantages. Here are four, two major and two minor:

1. Flip chart presentations offer a sense of understatement, subtlety, and intimacy that create just the right atmosphere for this type of meeting.

2. Using a flip chart demonstrates a certain amount of preparation, whereas anybody can quickly change a

few words in a computer-based presentation to suit an individual customer.

3. The lights stay on, so the focus is on people and eye contact is maintained.

4. A flip chart is not subject to the software and hardware glitches common with computer technology. And you don't have to worry about a lightbulb failure as you do with projectors. Incidentally, "BMI" is a global technology leader. Guess what BMI's account executive used in his presentations to Renard (and it wasn't PowerPoint)?

FOUR POINTS TO ENSURE A SUCCESSFUL PRESENTATION MEETING

Achieving success with the Business Presentation involves many factors. Distilling out the four most consistently present in the best presentations I've witnessed, here are my recommendations:

1. **Manage the meeting!** It bears repeating: The Business Presentation is not about delivering a speech, it's about managing a meeting. As with any meeting, you need to engage in a bit of warm-up chat, set a clear direction, manage the discussion, and steer the meeting toward next steps.

   Juggling all these responsibilities is challenging for most salespeople. Before delivering the actual presentation, their nervous energy focuses on the stand-up part, the presentation itself. After delivering it, they breathe a sigh of relief and start to coast, giving insufficient attention to steering the meeting toward the next steps.

2. **Confirm, don't educate!** An important but often tricky element of your delivery is when you talk about your understanding of the customer's business issues and business direction. This challenges most salespeople because of the need to *confirm*, not educate or persuade, because salespeople think they always need to be persuasive and forceful in their presentations. The delivery of this "front-end confirmation" portion of the

THE BUSINESS PRESENTATION IS NOT ABOUT DELIVERING A SPEECH, IT'S ABOUT MANAGING A MEETING.

presentation requires the salesperson to take on a much different persona. Because the salesperson is confirming his or her understanding of the customer's business, he or she must use the kind of language to communicate that fact.

The mistake that many salespeople make is to sound as if they are *educating* the customer on the customer's own business. Instead, the salesperson should display knowledge and a credible understanding of the executive's world without appearing presumptuous or preachy. To do this effectively, use "wiggle words"— phrases that allow you to convey the right tone when confirming your view of the customer's world.

Paradoxically, wiggle words communicate to the customer that the salesperson takes seriously his or her desire to understand the customer's business. Here are some examples:

At the start of the front-end confirmation you might say, "I've done my best to understand your business before today's meeting, but I just want to make sure I got it right. May I take a minute to confirm my perceptions?"

Then as you move through that front-end, try using phrases such as:

"It's my understanding that . . . "
"One perception I have is that . . . "
"If I'm not mistaken . . . "
"We sense that . . . "
"It appears that . . . "
"You may be considering . . . "

Do this well when you talk to customers about their business situations, and you'll score countless Business Resource points.

3. **Execute transitions well!** The words, phrases, proper pauses, and the like that you employ to pass from one element of your presentation to the next profoundly affect its outcome. Practice your transitions from the

> THE SALESPERSON SHOULD DISPLAY KNOWLEDGE AND A CREDIBLE UNDERSTANDING OF THE EXECUTIVE'S WORLD WITHOUT APPEARING PRESUMPTUOUS OR PREACHY.

point at which you are sitting during the warm-up to the point at which you're going to stand and start the presentation.

Here's a hint: Don't say, "Should we get started now?" This kills the informal atmosphere you just built in the warm-up.

Practice the transition between every page of your presentation. Practice the transition from the "business fit" to your closing recommendations, and then the transition to returning to the table to retake your seat for continuing in discussion mode. One way to know if you have constructed your transitions seamlessly is to see if you can begin to introduce the next page of the presentation before you actually flip to that page.

4. **Rehearse! Rehearse! Rehearse!** While your objective is to manage a meeting and to be informal and conversational, you can't conduct a Business Presentation off-the-cuff. You don't want to appear rehearsed, but you do want to appear prepared and professional. Rehearse with an audience and/or a video camera. No professional athlete, musician, or actor performs before an audience without practice or rehearsal. Why wouldn't the same hold true for a business professional?

Rehearsing your presentation helps you develop the confidence necessary to be seen as executive credible because it helps you project in a comfortable, informal way. Ironically, only through formal rehearsal can a salesperson appear informal and unrehearsed.

"I don't want to over-rehearse" is the statement of an amateur.

> IRONICALLY, ONLY THROUGH FORMAL REHEARSAL CAN A SALESPERSON APPEAR INFORMAL AND UNREHEARSED.

THE RESULT? EXECUTIVE CREDIBILITY

Executive credibility is part of the DNA of the sales professional in the new era of selling. And much of that credibility comes from your competence with the Business Presentation. Your command of the customer's business,

SALES PROFESSIONALS WHO RECOGNIZE THESE REALITIES AND PUT THE BUSINESS PRESENTATION AT THE CORE OF THEIR ARSENAL ARE THE ONES WHO ULTIMATELY BREATHE THAT RAREFIED AIR OF THE WORLD-CLASS SALESPERSON IN THE REDEFINED WORLD OF SELLING.

your ability to position your company and value proposition, your ability to conceptualize and articulate a business fit, and your ability to steer the customer to the next steps all combine to earn you enormous executive-level credibility.

Succeeding in the new era of selling is about creating demand for your company by creating value for the customer company. But that value needs a communication vehicle. Sales professionals who recognize these realities and put the Business Presentation at the core of their arsenal are the ones who ultimately breathe that rarefied air of the world-class salesperson in the redefined world of selling.

chapter 8

"Atlanta is a Third World city."

—"How Atlanta Stole the Olympics," *Fortune,* July 22, 1996

PRAGMATIC POSITIONING

Let's say you were attempting to sell the city in which you live to the International Olympic Committee as a prime location to host the games.

You'd probably get busy promoting your city's strong infrastructure, highway system, communications network, low crime rate, skilled labor force, and the like. It certainly wouldn't be obvious to you to promote your city as one of the poorest, most crime-ridden, least-educated, worst-housed municipalities in the nation. Surely you wouldn't talk about your city's overloaded sewage system's dumping of tons of untreated waste into the local rivers and a state government that imposed a moratorium on new sewers.

Yet that's exactly what Andy Young and Billy Payne did. They're the two who orchestrated Atlanta's successful bid to host the 1996 Summer Games. Those attributes raised the city's score, not lowered it.

As *Fortune* reported it: "Astonishingly, when the time came to go out and bag an Olympics, Billy and Andy managed to turn their bleak story into a selling point. Remember, as our two heroes hit the road in search of Olympic votes, they had to overcome anti-American sentiment. And so, to a select but powerful bloc of IOC members, Billy and Andy sold Atlanta as a Third World city, as the capital of African America—as, in fact, the only African city in the running for the games."

What Payne and Young used so successfully to bag the '96 Summer Games is a textbook example of Positioning: Concentrating on a theme that defines your company and its message in the mind of the customer. In this chapter, I briefly address why, in the new era of selling, Positioning is even more important than it's ever been. But the bulk of what I cover here is dedicated to showing you a practical approach for integrating Positioning into your sales process.

Positioning: The Total Sales Plan's Missing Link

To be sure, sales campaigns are won without Positioning. Many are won almost exclusively on the strength of the seller's ability to demonstrate knowledge of the customer's business. Likewise, many have been won on the basis of demonstrating the most compelling value proposition among competing suppliers. And many sales deals are won as a result of the sheer political savvy of a sales rep's astutely working the organizational dynamics within the buying company, which perhaps compensates for an inferior value proposition.

Customer business knowledge, value proposition, and political strategy—these are three pieces of a total sales plan that individually or in combination can frequently get the job done. But all three would have fallen short in the case of Atlanta's quest to snag an Olympic event. Indeed, Atlanta's "value proposition" couldn't have been weaker.

The missing element is the fourth and final piece of a total sales plan: Positioning, which needs to play a prominent role for salespeople who want to succeed in selling's new business model.

The concept of Positioning sounds simple enough. And it is. In fact, most salespeople are familiar with it on an intuitive level and put it to use to varying degrees. But

What Payne and Young used so successfully to bag the '96 Summer Games is a textbook example of Positioning: Concentrating on a theme that defines your company and its message in the mind of the customer.

Positioning needs to be implemented more consciously and consistently, especially by those endangered species who continue to focus on communicating information to customers as the central element of their sales "strategy."

Value must be positioned, not just described. Business-to-business salespeople need to borrow a page from the world of consumer marketing. Where marketers say, Coke is "The Real Thing," salespeople might be prone to say something like, Coke is "The world's best mixture of corn syrup, caramel color, and carbonated water." Likewise, marketers say, it's "The Softer Side of Sears," not, again as salespeople might say, "Sears' new line of clothing and other non-hardware goods."

Mel, a salesperson for a client of mine, was selling inventory control software to a large feed mill company. Mel's competitor's product was clearly superior to his on a feature-by-feature comparison. Its value proposition was much more compelling, especially for this customer.

But Mel's company had one feed mill installation already under its belt; his competitor had none. Throughout the sales campaign Mel never deviated from his Positioning message: his company's "feed mill expertise." Unlike many salespeople, Mel never let his competitor suck him into a feature battle. By staying "on message," Mel won the deal.

"The Real Thing" and "The Softer Side of Sears" are positioning messages that probably cost their companies many millions of dollars to develop and tapped the expertise of some of the best marketing minds in business at the time. Countless books have been written on the subject. Corporate America spends billions learning about and implementing Positioning. My goal in this book is to distill the essence of Positioning in a way that makes it practical for the business-to-business sales professional to use. That's why I call this chapter "Pragmatic Positioning."

Before we dig further into what Positioning is, let's address why it's important and how it brings value to customers. There are three reasons, all related, for why

VALUE MUST BE POSITIONED, NOT JUST DESCRIBED.

UNLIKE MANY SALESPEOPLE, MEL NEVER LET HIS COMPETITOR SUCK HIM INTO A FEATURE BATTLE. BY STAYING "ON MESSAGE," MEL WON THE DEAL.

Positioning is an essential, value-creating activity, and why its value is even greater in the redefined world of selling.

1. **Information overload.** The problem used to be customer ignorance—customers needed to be informed by salespeople. This situation, however, has inverted itself almost overnight. Today, customers have too much information. Customer *confusion* is the real problem. Positioning adds clarity and simplicity in a world that has become remarkably cluttered for buyers.

2. **People instinctively trust simplicity.** The great philosopher Dietrich von Hildebrand put it this way: "Truth bears the sign of a certain clear simplicity and directness and is harder to reach than are the varieties of error." Done right, Positioning affords customers the clear simplicity they can trust.

   Von Hildebrand continued, "The basic error of false simplicity lies in the assumption that it is a simple thing to have true simplicity." Indeed, Albert Einstein became *Time* magazine's Person of the Century on the strength of one very simple equation—$E=mc^2$ (energy equals mass times the speed of light squared). Yet beneath Einstein's theory of relativity lies massive complexity beyond the reach of most mortals.

   Any sales rep can rattle off reams of information. Good salespeople can summarize that information and even make it relevant to specific customers. Great salespeople take that information and use it to position a message, concentrating on a simple theme. This is much more complex than just communicating useful information.

3. **Customers don't really know why they buy.** For years this notion has shown up in books on selling, together with various psychological explanations. Bottom line: customers tend to make decisions for any number of emotional or personal reasons and then look for a business rationale to legitimize the personal reason.

This phenomenon is becoming even more pervasive because information overload is getting worse by the day. To help customers make their buying decisions, sales reps need to give customers the business rationale, and do so in a way that captures the essence of the sales rep's own, well-positioned value proposition.

Remember what Andy Grove said back in 1996 about selling in the future? "Salespeople are not going to be involved in information flow at the most basic level." Positioning is the antithesis of basic information flow.

THE ART OF WAR: 101

The essence of Pragmatic Positioning is Competitive Engagement, which can be defined as the science of developing and communicating a message based on yours and your competitors' strengths and weaknesses. Not only must you do your job to try to win the customer, but you must also take responsibility for making your competition lose.

NOT ONLY MUST YOU DO YOUR JOB TO TRY TO WIN THE CUSTOMER, BUT YOU MUST ALSO TAKE RESPONSIBILITY FOR MAKING YOUR COMPETITION LOSE.

Competitive Engagement is deceptively simple: "Go where they ain't." It's the nuances of implementation that make it hard. But most sales pros internalize effective Competitive Engagement pretty quickly once they are armed with an awareness of some of its specifics, the constant desire to use it, and a little trial and error.

The elements of Competitive Engagement owe their birth to a general in the Chinese army who lived more than twenty-five hundred years ago. Sun Tzu and his principles are embodied in a remarkably thin, simple, and readable book, *The Art of War*. The book got a new life when U.S. troops waiting to go to war with Iraq in 1990 and 1991 were seen reading it.

COMPETITIVE ENGAGEMENT IS DECEPTIVELY SIMPLE: "GO WHERE THEY AIN'T."

Sun Tzu's principles continue to influence modern warfare and competitive engagements in other walks of life as well, politics and marketing, for example. Some sales consulting firms and training companies have created versions of Competitive Engagement based on the Chinese general's work. One good example is found in Jim Holden's book, *Power Base Selling* (Wiley).

Consider these aphorisms of Sun Tzu, which have withstood the test of more than two millennia, and see if you can't immediately see how appropriate they are to selling:

- "He will win who knows when to fight and when not to fight."
- "We are not fit to lead an army unless we are familiar with the face of the country."
- "Your strength will eventually become your weakness."
- "Though the enemy may be stronger in numbers, we may prevent him from fighting."
- "The opportunity of defeating the enemy is provided by the enemy himself."
- "He will win who knows how to handle both superior and inferior forces."
- "If you know the enemy and know yourself, you need not fear the result of a hundred battles."
- "If the enemy's forces are united, separate them."

Sun Tzu's Two Methods of Engagement

Sun Tzu says, "In battle, there are not more than two methods of attack, the direct and the indirect; yet these two in combination give rise to an endless series of maneuvers."

I won't discuss an endless series of maneuvers. Instead, I'll simply illustrate a few practical applications of Sun Tzu's Direct and Indirect methods of attack as they relate to engaging competition in sales situations:

1. Sun Tzu's First Method of Attack: Direct

"It is the rule in war if our forces are five to the enemy's one, to attack him."   —Sun Tzu

As a salesperson, you'll use a Direct method when you have clear superiority over the competition, that is, when you dominate the competition. Your clear superiority over your competition must be in the mind of your *customer*,

SUN TZU SAYS, "IN BATTLE, THERE ARE NOT MORE THAN TWO METHODS OF ATTACK, THE DIRECT AND THE INDIRECT; YET THESE TWO IN COMBINATION GIVE RISE TO AN ENDLESS SERIES OF MANEUVERS."

not in yours. It's not uncommon for salespeople to become so enamored of their own product that they mistakenly assume their prospective customer views their offering through those same rose-colored glasses.

As an illustration of the Direct method, consider a scene from the comic adventure movie *Crocodile Dundee*, the story of a fellow from the Australian Outback who pays a visit to New York City. As Dundee and the film's leading lady walk arm-in-arm along a city street, a thug jumps out from behind a pillar, brandishing a dagger. The woman cautions Dundee to be careful, since the mugger has a knife. Sneers Dundee, "That ain't no knife. *This* is a knife," and he pulls from his boot a weapon with an 18-inch blade. Of course, the thug throws down his own puny little knife and flees.

In another example, one of my clients is a financial software company whose product was generally positioned as an enterprise solution for smaller companies ($50 million to $200 million in revenues). They had made it to the finals in a competitive battle to win the business of a $50 million prospect. The other software company in the finals offered a business version of a highly popular personal financial software package.

In this case, the appropriate method of engagement for our client was Direct, illustrating its sheer dominance by comparing its product feature by feature with the competition's. My client was able to draw its competitor into this arena and slay the competitor with something of a "death from a thousand features."

You would also use a form of a Direct method of engagement when you face a competitor who has a long-standing relationship with the target company or your goal is to pursue a particular application in which your company is strong but your competitor has either no interest in providing or no ability to do so.

Here's an example from the world of marketing. A print ad placed by Canon appeared in numerous publications in 1998. It read:

It's not uncommon for salespeople to become so enamored of their own product that they mistakenly assume their prospective customer views their offering through those same rose-colored glasses.

70% of Canon digital copiers sold in 1998 were connected to a network.

Only 15% of Xerox copiers were.

When it comes to networked digital copiers, the clear choice is Canon.

Imagine for a minute if Canon had attempted to position itself as the dominant player in the entire copier market. Its ad would have exhibited some form of this assertion: "Canon copiers are better than Xerox copiers," a message not likely to carry much credibility. On the other hand, when Canon carves out the networked digital niche of the copier market, the company is able to show clear superiority.

One of my clients, a firm that provides CRM (or customer relationship management) software, was competing with one of the biggest players in its market space to win the business of a large brokerage house. Only these two competitors remained on the prospect's final shortlist, something of a David-and-Goliath battle. Eventually, the David company had the objectivity and courage to acknowledge to itself that it was outgunned. Rather than "go down fighting"—an outcome it knew to be inevitable if it continued—the company chose to concede the lion's share of the business to the Goliath. However, the David company brought into sharp focus the prospect's urgent need for a Web-based customer service solution, which, of course, it offered but which its competitor was at least another year away from being able to deliver. My client's execution of the Direct method of engagement worked, and David and Goliath are coexisting at the same account.

2. Sun Tzu's Second Method of Attack: Indirect

"Appear where you are not expected."—Sun Tzu

Some derivative of a Direct method of engagement is appropriate only when you have sheer dominance over the competition, for all or part of a customer's need. Few companies command such superiority that customers

SOME DERIVATIVE OF A DIRECT METHOD OF ENGAGEMENT IS APPROPRIATE ONLY WHEN YOU HAVE SHEER DOMINANCE OVER THE COMPETITION, FOR ALL OR PART OF A CUSTOMER'S NEED.

instantly recognize, especially these days when product superiority seems to disappear in a nanosecond. In such cases, Sun Tzu's second method of engagement is called for: Indirect.

Recall a famous scene from the film *Raiders of the Lost Ark*. Indiana Jones has just used a whip with considerable skill to fend off a few villains when he comes face-to-face with a man equally skilled but with a three-foot sword, which he twirls in front of Jones. The audience watches in eager anticipation of an interesting but apparently fair battle: sword against whip. Instead, Jones suddenly pulls out his revolver and shoots his opponent.

One key to implementing the Indirect method of engagement is timing. If Indiana Jones makes it known that he intends to use a revolver in this confrontation, his opponent would not be so foolish as to engage in the battle.

So it goes in selling. When you're about to change the ground rules in a sales campaign, you should almost always do it late in the sales cycle to prevent the competition from adjusting. The exception occurs when the competition has no remotely credible way of pulling a "we can do that, too" counterattack. In my earlier example of Mel's selling his inventory control software to a feed mill client, his focusing on "feed mill expertise" when his competition had no feed mill installations shows his use of an Indirect method of engagement. The established ground rules had been that of feature richness, not feed mill experience. Because his competition had no such experience, Mel knew he should present his message of "feed mill expertise" early and often rather than waiting until the last minute to change the ground rules.

Also remember the obvious: "Go where they ain't!" As you size up your selling situation and your competition, ask yourself how you can lead with a perceived strength of your own against a perceived weakness of your competition. Here's an illustration of an Indirect method of engagement from the world of management consulting.

The consulting firm Coopers & Lybrand placed a series of print ads that showed a large picture of an ancient Chinese sword. The ad's caption read, "Does your consultant quote *The Art of War* but shy away from battle?" Coopers & Lybrand was attempting to change the ground rules for the purchase of management consulting services from "providing theoretical strategic advice" (quoting *The Art of War*) to "facilitating the *implementation* of strategy" (engaging in the "battle")—something its competitors are not particularly strong at doing.

One can even use an Indirect method when responding to a Request for Proposal (RFP). Figure 8-1 shows how a proposal cover letter did just that.

A highly structured "sealed bid" Request for Proposal from a very large industrial company solicited proposals for its natural gas supply. As is true with most RFPs, the requesting company in this case planned to compare proposals from multiple gas suppliers and select the lowest-price offering. But my client's sales pro had different plans for her response to the RFP. Julie changed the ground rules from quoting the "lowest wellhead price"—the measure typically used to compare natural gas prices that the Request for Proposal contained—to quoting "total energy cost," and she won the deal. Unlike Mel's feed mill case, Julie's last-minute timing was essential to prevent her competitors from attempting the same approach. (See Figure 8-1, page 151.)

Another situation in which you would implement an Indirect method of engagement is when you're losing or you've lost. When it becomes clear that the customer is going to buy from your competition, whether because your offering just isn't as strong or because you've been otherwise outsold, your only option is to attempt to delay the purchase altogether.

This derivative of the Indirect method relies, in part, on sowing FUD—Fear, Uncertainty, and Doubt. It centers on communicating a message that says if the customer waits

ANOTHER SITUATION IN WHICH YOU WOULD IMPLEMENT AN INDIRECT METHOD OF ENGAGEMENT IS WHEN YOU'RE LOSING OR YOU'VE LOST.

Mr. Christopher P. Jones
U.S. Heavy Industries, Inc.
123 Old Toll Road
Westport, CT 06880

Dear Mr. Jones:

In response to your Request for Proposal (RFP No. 6B007FKP), KPS Energy Services, Inc. (KPSES), is pleased to submit the enclosed proposal to USHI for your energy requirements. We trust that you will find that our proposal responds to all of the issues identified in your RFP.

We would like to take a moment to comment on the approach we have taken in our proposal, and on KPSES' business philosophy in general.

One approach, commonly adopted by most energy suppliers, is to submit an artificially low price for initial wellhead supplies in order to appear to have competitive pricing, then make up associated losses through so-called "incidental" fees and by passing on various risks and penalty charges to the customer. Some of these fees and charges can dwarf any apparent savings the customer might have received from the original wellhead commodity pricing. While that approach seems to have become a nearly standard energy industry practice, it is not KPS Energy Services' approach.

Instead, we embrace a *total energy cost* reduction methodology. Our customers, including the references enclosed with our proposal, prefer this because they find it reduces their overall energy cost and eliminates surprises. Many of these surprises occur in the areas of balancing and cash-out penalties, capacity utilization charges, incremental supply pricing fees, and delivery curtailment during very cold periods. We believe that this business philosophy is one of the reasons that KPSES was recently voted number one in "dependability in agreements and commitments" in a recent independent national survey of over one hundred energy suppliers. We hope that USHI will review our proposal in this context.

Chris, thank you for considering KPSES to be your energy resource. We look forward to meeting with you to discuss further how we can be an important part of your team. In the meantime, please call us if we can clarify any components of our proposal.

Sincerely,

Julie M. Ellison

Enclosure

Fig. 8-1
EXAMPLE OF IMPLEMENTING AN INDIRECT METHOD OF ENGAGEMENT IN AN RFP RESPONSE

just a little longer to make a decision, the seller will be able to provide a solution far superior to the one currently under consideration or at a far more attractive price, or will otherwise offer some significant benefit to the customer who delays or changes the buying decision.

In December 1998, for example, Hitachi Data Systems placed a number of ads to promote its soon-to-be-released Skyline II computer. Several lines of text in those ads said that Hitachi's Skyline I was currently the fastest computer in the world. The main caption of the ad said:

> During 3Q '99, the fastest mainframe on the planet will be moving almost two times faster. Look to the Skyline II.

It's interesting that at the same time this ad appeared in late 1998 and early 1999, IBM was releasing its latest box, whose speed eclipsed that of Hitachi's Skyline I. Clearly, Hitachi was attempting to encourage customers to delay their purchase of a computer for just a few quarters, at which time Hitachi would be able to deliver an even faster machine than the new IBM.

Here's another example, one from a client of mine, JBM, Incorporated (not their real name), that sells regulatory compliance and safety solutions to a wide range of industries, primarily to the trucking and transportation industry. A large national charitable organization found itself in need of a safety compliance solution whose cost was in the range of $300,000. My client's competitor changed the ground rules, proposing at the last minute to provide the solution as a charitable donation to the agency. The agency promptly agreed to the arrangement.

JBM had to stop the deal—and fast. Its only hope was to plant a seed of doubt in the customer's mind that despite its competitor's good intentions, that company was incapable of fulfilling the agency's requirements and would leave the agency even more exposed to citations, fines, and bad press. This projection was, in fact, true.

CLEARLY, HITACHI WAS ATTEMPTING TO ENCOURAGE CUSTOMERS TO DELAY THEIR PURCHASE OF A COMPUTER FOR JUST A FEW QUARTERS, AT WHICH TIME HITACHI WOULD BE ABLE TO DELIVER AN EVEN FASTER MACHINE THAN THE NEW IBM.

JBM's competitor had recently dismantled the very department that would have implemented the solution just accepted by the agency as a donation. This fact was known at the time to only a few inside players in JBM's industry.

The problem for JBM, as is so often the case, was *how* to plant the seed of doubt. Calling the regular contacts would not have worked, because none of them would have had the political stomach to run the issue up the chain of command. Nor would phoning the agency's senior management, because it's unlikely my client would get through. If it did, the agency's executive would most likely dismiss the call as sour grapes.

JBM also needed a paper trail, a gun that would lie dormant until another serious regulatory violation occurred, at which time that gun would smoke like a pile of burning tires. The letter shown in Figure 8-2 would be that smoking gun, and it would sit in the agency's file cabinet. For these reasons a letter to the executive was the most effective way to implement JBM's Indirect method.

There's another point to this example that bears mentioning: JBM's execution of its method of engagement was *not* done solely for the benefit of JBM, though my client did benefit. The customer benefited, too, perhaps even more than JBM, by avoiding the consequences of choosing a solution doomed to fail. I point this out to illustrate that "great selling"—certainly the case in this example—benefits both seller *and* buyer. (See Figure 8-2, page 154.)

> "GREAT SELLING"— CERTAINLY THE CASE IN THIS EXAMPLE—BENEFITS BOTH SELLER *AND* BUYER.

MORE ON IMPLEMENTING POSITIONING

Just before the November 1992 election, as then-candidate Bill Clinton departed Florida after inspecting the damage of a recent hurricane, he told the press, "I will not politicize this situation. I'll keep my criticism of how President Bush is handling the situation to myself."

In a similar vein, Allison, a Business Resource–level salesperson for another client of mine, was conducting her presentation to a buying committee for her company's

Mr. Jimmy D. Smith
Senior Vice President
Transportation Services
Major U.S. Charity
16 West 42nd Street
New York, NY 10017

Dear Mr. Smith:

Recently we were contacted by Major U.S. Charity's Transportation Services (MUSCTS) with a request to support your efforts to address several Federal Motor Carrier noncompliance issues that were discovered by MUSC's outside legal counsel. After reviewing your RFP, we responded with a proposal that outlines the approach of JBM, Incorporated, to bringing MUSCTS into compliance with the regulations (known as Federal Motor Carrier Safety Regulations).

Because of the scope of MUSCTS' operations and the number of years of noncompliance, the task is, frankly, not a trivial one. So when we heard a few days ago that a truckers' advocacy and lobbying group, the National Truck Drivers Association (NTDA), was going to attempt to perform the work as a charitable contribution, we were quite naturally puzzled.

While we recognize and respect the intentions and abilities of the NTDA (they're effective lobbyists and they're also a JBM customer), we believe the scope of the project far exceeds the range of any lobbying group, however well-intentioned.

That's why we are writing to request a brief meeting with you and, if appropriate, the key members of MUSCTS' management team. The purpose of the meeting is to both establish JBM's unique qualifications and to suggest alternative approaches that allow MUSC to benefit from NTDA's desire to make a contribution, yet still ensure a successful outcome of your compliance effort.

By way of introduction, JBM, Incorporated, is over 60 years old with more than 1,000 employees, all dedicated solely to safety and regulatory compliance. Our customer base is 200,000 strong and includes 90 percent of the Fortune 500. We are proud to be considered by most as "the source" for regulatory and compliance solutions.

Jimmy, we hope you will consider our request to review this issue with you directly. I'll call Ms. Kathy Hampton within the next few days in anticipation of scheduling a brief meeting with you. In the meantime if you would like to contact me, my telephone number is 1-800-555-3174, extension 2866.

Respectfully,

Robert J. O'Laughlin

Enclosure

Fig. 8-2

EXAMPLE OF IMPLEMENTING AN INDIRECT METHOD OF ENGAGEMENT
TO STOP A PURCHASE FROM A COMPETITOR

financial software. She told the committee, "It may surprise you to hear me say this, but our software is *not* robust out of the box, and that's by design." [Out of the box is a software package's ability to be functional immediately upon installation, without further programming.]

Allison then added, "We figure you don't have cookie-cutter problems, and you probably don't want a cookie-cutter solution. That's why we wouldn't dream of asking you to re-engineer your business in order to conform to the needs of an inflexible software solution."

Allison said what she said because her chief competitor's strength was its software's ability to function right out of the box. However, this strength exposed the customer to having to conform its operation to that vendor's inflexible software package—exactly what Allison wanted the customer to infer.

Bill Clinton and Allison both understand another aspect of Positioning: how to subtly put the competition on the defensive, and do it in a professional, innocuous way.

The Business Resource, as a display of supreme confidence that a customer will always be best off doing business with him or her, takes personal responsibility for making competitors lose. Putting the competition on the defensive is a key tactic to achieving that end.

This must be done with great care, of course. Word choice, timing, and your own credibility are just a few of the considerations. Imagine if Bill Clinton had said, "I don't think President Bush is doing enough to help the hurricane victims. If I were president, I would . . . ." He would have been accused of politicizing a tragedy, thereby losing favor with voters.

If Allison had said, "You don't want software with out-of-the-box strength, it won't have the flexibility you need," she would have been suspected of trying to mask her own product's weaknesses.

Let's say you're up against a company that's well-known for giving steep, last-minute discounts. For example, here's what Hector did when he found himself facing his arch

ANOTHER ASPECT OF POSITIONING: HOW TO SUBTLY PUT THE COMPETITION ON THE DEFENSIVE, AND DO IT IN A PROFESSIONAL, INNOCUOUS WAY.

rival, after the two of them made it to the final cut in a highly competitive battle for a CRM software solution. The competitor was well-known for its tactic of offering the prospect big, last-minute discounts on its software.

Hector knew he didn't want to be drawn into a pricing war that nobody wins. So he manufactured a relatively minor issue that would require a brief, one-on-one meeting with the customer. After meeting with the person he'd tagged as the most influential member of the buying team and clarifying the minor "issue," Hector carefully made what appeared as an innocuous comment during their "small talk" as the two men walked to the lobby:

> Incredibly, there are still a few companies left in our industry that use that old, worn-out tactic of offering a steep, last-minute discount on their software and then make up the losses in the service and support area after the sale. The rest of us in the industry have seen most of these companies go out of business and have bets on how soon the remaining few will drop.
>
> I should tell you in advance that if our competitor on this opportunity is one of those few companies, my company will not counter their offer, since it would force us to also cut back on after-sales service and support!

THE COMPETITOR DID JUST WHAT HECTOR PREDICTED. HIS COMPANY DID NOT MATCH THE COMPETITOR'S LAST-MINUTE DISCOUNT—AND IT WON THE BUSINESS.

The competitor did just what Hector predicted. His company did not match the competitor's last-minute discount—and it won the business. If Hector hadn't actively, but oh so subtly, created an atmosphere that put his competitor on the defensive, he would have had great difficulty avoiding the appearance of selling overpriced software.

WORDS ARE EVERYTHING

For Pragmatic Positioning to work, it must be executed with remarkable attention to word choice. It's the words you use that make the technique come to life. Salespeople need to pay closer attention to how they say what they say—because, contrary to popular belief, the ear trumps the eye when it comes to fixing a picture in someone's mind. Sales professionals need to become less concerned with having sexy slides and graphics to convey their message and more concerned with finding the right word or words to create that picture in the customer's mind.

What picture could possibly create the same effect as the words: "The softer side of Sears?" A picture can only describe a reality. A word can create it.

Your success in implementing Pragmatic Positioning rises or falls with the words you use. The wrong choice of word in the most subtle of contexts can doom a positioning message. Determining which method of Competitive Engagement to use is not the hard part—it's choosing the right words in the right situations to *implement* the method of engagement.

To take a simple example, compare two hypothetical candidates for U.S. president. One says, "If elected, I will propose to Congress ten billion dollars in Medicare cuts." The other vows, "If elected, I will propose to Congress ten billion dollars in Medicare savings." Both have said the identical thing, but each will be viewed differently by the same voter.

Indeed, a single letter in a word can sometimes make a profound difference. Consider Jhane Barnes, one of the world's premier fashion designers. Her name had originally been spelled Jane Barnes. But as *USA Today* reported on August 10, 2000, "Barnes lost sales after retailers learned she wasn't a man. The main reason she altered her first name was to make her logo appear both more masculine and European. To this day, some major customers still don't know how to pronounce it."

USA Today went on to point out that Barnes acknowledges that her business would not have survived without the "h."

As you transform yourself into the Business Resource you want to be, you must migrate away from "communicating information" as the core of your value as a sales professional. You must instead "position a message." Only then can you bring maximum value to your own company and to your customers. Only then will you achieve world-class status in the new era of selling.

chapter 9

"You have to be willing to suck it up and walk away."

—A spokesperson for FedEx (referring to prospects and customers
his company doesn't want to pursue or keep),
The Wall Street Journal, January 7, 1999

OPPORTUNITY ASSESSMENT

In selling's old business model, "great selling" generally referred to the ability to sell anything to anyone—freezers to Eskimos, as the saying goes. The essence of selling's new business model is expressed by the willingness of a senior executive at one of the largest freight companies in the United States to "suck it up." That one sound bite articulates what is without question one of the most difficult things for traditional salespeople to do: walk away from an "opportunity." Yet that very ability is a trademark of the Business Resource.

Stanley Gault, the legendary former CEO of Rubbermaid Company, used to visit hardware stores on weekends and check that the labels were placed properly on Rubbermaid containers. For him that small detail offered a quick, simple litmus test to see whether things were falling apart somewhere upstream in his company's production process.

In much the same way, if you want a quick read on a sales organization's effectiveness, ask what criteria it uses to determine how many resources to give to the pursuit of its various sales opportunities.

In this chapter, I describe the process and give you the criteria for measuring the true quality of a sales opportunity

IF YOU WANT A QUICK READ ON A SALES ORGANIZATION'S EFFECTIVENESS, ASK WHAT CRITERIA IT USES TO DETERMINE HOW MANY RESOURCES TO GIVE TO THE PURSUIT OF ITS VARIOUS SALES OPPORTUNITIES.

and then mapping that opportunity's quality against the resources needed to win it.

FROM QUALIFICATION TO OPPORTUNITY ASSESSMENT

The Business Resource looks for mutual value in sales situations, and does so by using *objective criteria*. That's why the Business Resource is confident in knowing when to walk away from an "opportunity." A Vendor/Problem-Solver tries to gauge how likely and how soon a prospect is going to buy, and does so by depending mostly on gut feelings.

The Business Resource can explain in concrete terms why she is or is not pursuing an opportunity and why she's willing to commit more, or fewer, resources, such as her own time and her company's other resources, to various sales situations. A Vendor/Problem-Solver assesses sales situations using criteria that range anywhere from a basic hunch to the only slightly more scientific question, "Do the opportunity's technical specifications meet the specifications of our solution, and is the customer ready to buy?"

Here is yet another major difference between a Business Resource and a Vendor/Problem-Solver: One conducts Opportunity Assessment, the other merely "qualifies deals."

Opportunity Assessment is one of the most important activities salespeople perform—and it's getting more important all the time. In the new business model of selling, the sales professional must be able to make judgments about what kind of relationship his or her company should have with customer companies, judgments that have profound implications.

For example, the Business Resource might recommend that her company pull back considerably on the resources it's giving to its biggest customer and establish instead a transactional type of relationship with that account, perhaps discontinuing having a salesperson call altogether. Such a recommendation made on gut feel could be catastrophic.

THE BUSINESS RESOURCE CAN EXPLAIN IN CONCRETE TERMS WHY SHE IS OR IS NOT PURSUING AN OPPORTUNITY AND WHY SHE'S WILLING TO COMMIT MORE, OR FEWER, RESOURCES, SUCH AS HER OWN TIME AND HER COMPANY'S OTHER RESOURCES, TO VARIOUS SALES SITUATIONS.

Historically, we've called the process of measuring a prospect's sales potential "qualification." The more complete term, Opportunity Assessment, spans the entire range of circumstances that salespeople face. At one end, Opportunity Assessment summarizes the basic questions that a salesperson must answer to determine whether or not a very specific and well-defined sales opportunity is worth a chase.

At the other end, Opportunity Assessment encompasses a very fundamental question that salespeople must answer—a question that's often more important than any related solely to the "deal" at hand: whether two companies ought to be doing business together at all, independent of specific opportunities, and what kind of relationship they should have. Seen from that vantage point, Opportunity Assessment addresses sweeping questions about how the selling company should deploy its resources.

Prior to engaging my firm, my clients, almost without exception, had been assigning their customers to channels or salespeople based on account size. They used the same basis for deploying their resources to their customers.

One of my clients who had done it this way for years gives us a particularly interesting example. A manufacturing company, it had more than 150,000 customers, ranging from Fortune 500 giants to ten-person shops. As this manufacturer began to internalize Opportunity Assessment, it realized that some of its biggest national accounts were actually some of its least profitable customers, who sought nothing more than a highly efficient, low-cost transactional relationship. Some of those customers all but refused to spend time with the salespeople so eager to "partner" with them.

Through Opportunity Assessment, this manufacturer realized that many of the mom-and-pop companies among its customers were actually seeking a high-value, integral relationship with it. A lot of these accounts, however, were being serviced by a highly transaction-oriented telesales rep who, by virtue of job description and not necessarily

OPPORTUNITY ASSESSMENT ADDRESSES SWEEPING QUESTIONS ABOUT HOW THE SELLING COMPANY SHOULD DEPLOY ITS RESOURCES.

skill, was unable to cultivate such a relationship or was largely unaware of the need to even explore the possibility.

Over time, this client rethought the very principles of its account assignment process. Today, some of the biggest companies in its customer base are e-commerce–only accounts, while some fairly puny companies are given surprising levels of attention and resources. Most important, each customer type is happiest this way, and my client has very few unacceptably low-margin customers.

JUST BECAUSE IT CAN FOG A MIRROR DOESN'T MEAN YOU SHOULD CHASE IT

Unlike qualification, the outcome of Opportunity Assessment doesn't yield a simple go/no-go decision. Instead, the Business Resource uses Opportunity Assessment as a tool *throughout* a sales campaign and throughout the life of a customer relationship to measure mutual value. The Business Resource then maps that mutual value against the resources needed to realize it.

That's why the Business Resource, unlike the Vendor/Problem-Solver, may be able to objectively justify pursuing a smaller opportunity while de-emphasizing a seemingly bigger one that is not, upon closer inspection, worth the effort.

> THE BUSINESS RESOURCE IS ALSO ABLE TO MAKE SURE THAT THOSE HIGH-RESOURCE-DRAINING, LOW-VALUE ACCOUNTS—THE CLASSIC "CUSTOMERS FROM HELL"—WIND UP IN THE LAP OF THE COMPETITION.

The Business Resource is also able to make sure that those high-resource-draining, low-value accounts—the classic "customers from hell"—wind up in the lap of the competition.

My firm conducted an informal study to quantify how salespeople parcel out time to their various sales opportunities. Although I don't claim that this survey meets all the demands of statistical validity, its results are consistent with the empirical observations of our firm's consultants from their hands-on work with our clients' salespeople: namely, that salespeople spend too much time on sure winners and sure losers and not enough time on sales situations whose outcomes are highly dependent on the salesperson's efforts.

We found, in retrospect, that most salespeople spend about twice as much time as they should on opportunities that they would have won with very little selling effort, and about the same amount of time on opportunities that they had almost no chance of winning, no matter how hard they sold.

That wasted time has to come from somewhere. The only place left is from those opportunities that, in retrospect, can be won or lost on the strength of the salesperson's efforts and effectiveness.

The halls of selling are littered with the skeletons of lost deals that only days before the defeat were "in the bag" . . . with the ghosts of prospects who, for many months, eagerly accepted your presales support on a complex solution, only to then send the thing out for bid . . . and with the echoes of two-thousand-dollar, face-to-face sales calls that would have served both companies better had they been two-dollar phone calls.

No one can afford such missteps today. Salespeople who refuse to take Opportunity Assessment seriously will be among the sales profession's earliest fatalities in the new era of selling.

Good Deals, Good Relationships, and How to Know If You've Found Them

I define a "sales opportunity" as a combination of (1) the specific sales opportunity—the deal at hand—and (2) the potential for a long-term relationship between the prospect and your company.

If the particular deal at hand looks like a good deal, and if the relationship potential involves the kind of company you want to do business with over the long haul, you have the two most relevant factors for determining the quality of a sales opportunity.

This determination of quality needs one more factor to enable you to effectively assess the value to you of that sales opportunity: the *resources* you and your company need to expend to win that sales opportunity and sustain that relationship.

The quality of the opportunity in relation to the expenditure of resources involved can be represented with a matrix that lets you categorize and evaluate individual sales opportunities as they arise.

QUALITY OF THE OPPORTUNITY	High Quality Low Resources	High Quality High Resources
	Low Quality Low Resources	Low Quality High Resources

RESOURCES NEEDED TO BE SUCCESSFUL

Fig. 9-1
THE OPPORTUNITY ASSESSMENT MATRIX

Figure 9-1 helps us distinguish among opportunities according to whether they represent High Quality/Low Resources (ideal); High Quality/High Resources; Low Quality/Low Resources; or Low Quality/High Resources (danger ahead!).

Such an approach removes from the driver's seat the traditional measures of opportunity quality used most commonly in making a decision to pursue: "size of the deal" or "size of the company." It gives us a far superior way to objectively answer the core questions we should always be asking ourselves about any sales opportunity:

- How hard should I pursue?
- How likely am I to win?
- How good will the business be?

Of particular note is the third core question: *How good will doing business with this prospect be?* Most salespeople

THE CORE QUESTIONS WE SHOULD ALWAYS BE ASKING OURSELVES ABOUT ANY SALES OPPORTUNITY:

- HOW HARD SHOULD I PURSUE?
- HOW LIKELY AM I TO WIN?
- HOW GOOD WILL THE BUSINESS BE?

pay lip service to this question but seldom let it influence their decision to pursue. Not so the Business Resource, who operates with a different mindset than traditional salespeople—and who even lets that difference be known to customers and prospects.

Consider the case of Rebecca, who sells software to large insurance companies. One customer was a California-based company that for more than four years used only one of her company's software products, a tertiary-level product, at that.

This customer was experiencing significant delays in its efforts to launch newly developed insurance products. Rebecca knew that if her company, using its technology, could work in conjunction with the customer's in-house I/S staff, the product launch problem would disappear. Problem was, the company's I/S staff followed a long-held tradition of "not invented here," and showed little interest in engaging an outside software company to assist in addressing its company's business challenges.

Despite this customer's aversion to using outsiders, Rebecca requested a Knowledge Call with a fairly influential midlevel manager in the I/S department, Kevin. The meeting was cordial, and Kevin was surprisingly forthcoming in the normal Knowledge Call dialogue. Yet he was clearly conveying an unspoken message of "we're not changing."

Very much a Business Resource, Rebecca took what most salespeople would consider a gutsy, if not potentially fatal, step during this call. She posed the following situation to Kevin in words similar to these:

> One of the reasons we wanted to meet with you today was to take a pulse of our business relationship and try to gauge how well our two companies' business philosophies match up, if they match at all. For as long as we've known your company, it's operated under a philosophy of doing most everything in-house. Yours is a successful company and, of course, we would never challenge that

HOW GOOD WILL DOING BUSINESS WITH THIS PROSPECT BE? MOST SALESPEOPLE PAY LIP SERVICE TO THIS QUESTION BUT SELDOM LET IT INFLUENCE THEIR DECISION TO PURSUE. NOT SO THE BUSINESS RESOURCE, WHO OPERATES WITH A DIFFERENT MINDSET THAN TRADITIONAL SALESPEOPLE.

philosophy; many successful companies operate in a similar way. It's just that my company fits best with companies that operate toward the other end of that philosophical spectrum, those that are favorably disposed to outsourcing so they can focus on their core competencies.

I'm sure you can understand the obligation we have to our customers to remain a healthy company. We know we'll remain a healthy company only if we invest in customer relationships that fit well with our business philosophy. Now, we're trying to make some decisions—potentially tough decisions—relative to how we should view the business relationship between our two companies as we look toward the future.

Rebecca paused only long enough to breathe before continuing, when Kevin—at first clearly taken aback by Rebecca's remarkably direct comments—suddenly changed his demeanor. The wall he'd been so careful to keep between the two companies seemed to disappear. What followed left Rebecca almost speechless: Kevin suggested she contact his internal business customer, something Kevin had never given her company the nod to do, despite many requests.

It was as if that brief exchange made Kevin stop seeing Rebecca as "another vendor" and instead start seeing her as a Business Resource who truly meant business . . . as if he could see she was both determined and able to make something work between the two companies . . . as if he'd be better off, politically, being associated with her instead of the one who tried keeping her out, because he knew she'd get in eventually.

Rebecca's experience illustrates yet another Business Resource principle. "The customer is always right" may be a noble customer service philosophy, but it's not a sales philosophy. The Business Resource takes personally the stewardship of his or her company resources. The Business Resource seeks only profitable, mutually valuable business relationships. What's more, customers know this.

"THE CUSTOMER IS ALWAYS RIGHT" MAY BE A NOBLE CUSTOMER SERVICE PHILOSOPHY, BUT IT'S NOT A SALES PHILOSOPHY. THE BUSINESS RESOURCE TAKES PERSONALLY THE STEWARDSHIP OF HIS OR HER COMPANY RESOURCES.

OPPORTUNITY ASSESSMENT CRITERIA

Let's recall the three factors we've been discussing: whether the particular deal at hand looks like a good deal, whether the relationship potential involves the kind of company you want to do business with over the long haul, and what resources you and your company need to expend to win and sustain that sales opportunity.

With this basic framework, we can now talk about the key criteria for Opportunity Assessment. These criteria apply to most selling environments.

QUALITY OF THE SPECIFIC SALES OPPORTUNITY

The quality of the Specific Sales Opportunity—the deal at hand—can be assessed by answering the following three basic questions:

1. **How real is it, and how soon will it happen?** Among the first lessons a salesperson learns from the school of hard knocks is the embarrassment of putting a ton of time and resources into an "opportunity" that exists only in the mind of a lightweight contact who is merely kicking tires.

    To know how real a specific sales opportunity is, you need two things: contacts who can be trusted to give you reliable information, and the guts to ask the questions. It's a good idea to get more than one person's perspective, too. Only Vendors wear rose-colored glasses; the Business Resource prefers 20/20 vision.

2. **What's the deal's short- and long-term revenue potential?** This question is usually the first one salespeople focus on, though it's easy to be misled by looking only at the short term. Is there ongoing business potential?

    It's important to look at the opportunity's profit potential. Unfortunately, it's not that easy. Assessing the profitability of business is a key *outcome* of Opportunity Assessment and requires that we complete the process.

AMONG THE FIRST LESSONS A SALESPERSON LEARNS FROM THE SCHOOL OF HARD KNOCKS IS THE EMBARRASSMENT OF PUTTING A TON OF TIME AND RESOURCES INTO AN "OPPORTUNITY" THAT EXISTS ONLY IN THE MIND OF A LIGHTWEIGHT CONTACT WHO IS MERELY KICKING TIRES.

3. **Does the deal offer marketing visibility for you?** Is this a marquee deal that can establish you as *the* provider of this product or solution? Is this a deal that can establish you in an industry you're trying to crack? In short, is this a deal that, if closed, is likely to lead to other business for you because of its endorsement quality?

QUALITY OF THE POTENTIAL BUSINESS RELATIONSHIP

The quality of the Potential Business Relationship can be assessed by answering the question, "What's the lifetime value—qualitative and quantitative—to my company of having this customer?" Said another way, "Is this really the type of company we want to do business with?"

Consider the story of Ron, a salesperson for a client of mine, a technology-based company. Ron suggested an account that would be perfect for a "partnership" (Ron's term) with his company. For more than a year he'd been trying to land this account, a major manufacturer of hand tools and hardware. Ron had an excellent contact at the prospect company, Alex, a true coach (again, Ron's term).

The day Ron made his first Knowledge Call on him (all of his previous calls had been traditional sales calls), Alex greeted Ron in the lobby and took him to a nearby "vendor meeting room." This was the first sign of trouble. Nevertheless, Ron went ahead to position the Knowledge Call with all the right sound bites.

He said, "Alex, it's our philosophy that the better we understand your business, the more value we can bring to you. We're on a homework mission here."

"That sounds fine," Alex replied.

One of the first steps in a Knowledge Call, as you may recall from Chapter 3, is to get a thorough understanding of both the formal and informal organizational structure of the customer, typically by asking the contact to help fill in the gaps of an impromptu hand-drawn organization chart. But when Ron attempted this, Alex froze up.

THE QUALITY OF THE POTENTIAL BUSINESS RELATIONSHIP CAN BE ASSESSED BY ANSWERING THE QUESTION, "WHAT'S THE LIFETIME VALUE—QUALITATIVE AND QUANTITATIVE—TO MY COMPANY OF HAVING THIS CUSTOMER?"

"We have a corporate policy against sharing any information about our company with suppliers, including information about who reports to whom," he said.

The purported Knowledge Call was over. It had lasted all of fifteen minutes—including the ten minutes of warm-up.

It was a good lesson, and all the more useful to Ron, who had unceremoniously dismissed the concept of "philosophical fit" when it had first been presented to his company's sales force. At that time Ron had said, "It sounds like you're saying that if, for example, our customer's building is brown, we should be saying to the customer, 'Gosh, your building is brown, Mr. Customer, and so is ours; therefore, our two companies fit philosophically and should do business together.' "

Of course, that's not what it is at all. As Ron learned, there are objective criteria for measuring the quality of a potential relationship between two companies. "Philosophical fit" is just another way of referring to the quality of that potential business relationship.

Here are six of the more reliable criteria:

1. **Information sharing.** How openly does this company share strategic information about itself with suppliers? This, of course, was at the heart of the philosophical misalignment between Ron's and Alex's companies. If you've been in sales for any length of time, you've probably witnessed firsthand how many companies talk about partnerships with suppliers yet refuse to share information. For them, "partnership" is merely a euphemism for getting the lowest price.

2. **Core competency focus.** Is this company attempting to focus only on what it does best, or does it try to do everything internally? How much, if at all, is it currently outsourcing? One very large and highly successful Minneapolis-based manufacturing company—a favorite target for salespeople—is philosophically misaligned for partnerships with almost any prospective supplier. It has

THERE ARE OBJECTIVE CRITERIA FOR MEASURING THE QUALITY OF A POTENTIAL RELATIONSHIP BETWEEN TWO COMPANIES.

a "company store" philosophy. This manufacturer has its own doctors and nurses and pharmacists, even its own interior design department for designing office layouts.

It's not that this philosophy is bad—the company in question is wildly successful—it's just that those aren't the usual trademarks of a company seeking to focus only on its core strengths. If it had such a focus, it would be a more suitable candidate for mutually valuable relationships with suppliers.

SALESPEOPLE MUST
MOVE BEYOND THE
AMBIGUOUS NOTION OF
WHETHER A COMPANY
IS A "PRICE BUYER"
OR "VALUE BUYER."
INSTEAD, TRY VIEWING
IT THIS WAY: DOES THE
COMPANY FOCUS ON UNIT
PRICE OR TOTAL COST
OF OWNERSHIP?

3. **Purchasing philosophy.** Salespeople must move beyond the ambiguous notion of whether a company is a "price buyer" or "value buyer." Instead, try viewing it this way: Does the company focus on unit price or total cost of ownership? A unit price company simply compares the cost of red widgets from several suppliers, figuring that all red widgets are created equal.

At the other end of the spectrum are companies that measure the total value of supplier relationships and "total cost of ownership." They're truly implementing strategic sourcing. They understand that the purchasing process itself costs a lot of money, as does maintaining relationships with suppliers. Most important, they understand that a product's "initial cost"—the price of the product that customers use to compare multiple vendors—is often a fraction of the product's total cost to them, the customer.

Consider, for example, software products. The total cost of installing and owning the software can exceed the initial price by a factor of more than ten, because of variables such as programming costs, process interruptions or redesigns, effects on customer inventory, and the like. Yet too many buyers of software pay only lip service to this fact. Salespeople need to spot such companies.

One indication of a company's purchasing philosophy is whether it is attempting to reduce its supplier base, a popular trend in corporate America for some time now.

In short, does the company see intrinsic value in its suppliers, or does it have a reputation for "vendor bashing?"

4. **Senior management involvement.** If senior executives never meet with suppliers, the company probably views suppliers as merely "vendors-on-demand," as in: "Wait at the door, I'll jerk your chain when I need you!" Companies whose senior executives take the time to meet with suppliers send a message that they value supplier relationships.

5. **Philosophy toward their customers.** A prospective customer that's a prime candidate for a high-mutual-value relationship with its suppliers is usually one that is also attempting to do the same thing with its own customers. One word of caution, though: Look for evidence of this, not just slogans, plaques, and bumper stickers about "loving customers."

6. **Culture and personality.** This is basic "chemistry." It's hard to define, but like so many things, you know it when you see it, and you definitely know when it's missing. Does the company seem to share your company's values? Does it view the role of technology, for example, similarly to the way your company does?

RESOURCES NEEDED FOR SUCCESS

Knowing the quality of a sales opportunity has value only if you also know what resources are likely to be required for you to snag that opportunity: How winnable is it and at what price—especially compared to other opportunities?

Here are nine useful criteria to help you anticipate the resources you'll have to deploy to succeed in closing that opportunity and sustaining the business relationship.

1. **Your support from powerful people.** Your sales plan is only as strong as the people who support it. Demonstrate your own sales savvy by avoiding the

KNOWING THE QUALITY OF A SALES OPPORTUNITY HAS VALUE ONLY IF YOU ALSO KNOW WHAT RESOURCES ARE LIKELY TO BE REQUIRED FOR YOU TO SNAG THAT OPPORTUNITY.

When you have support from powerful people, you will find sales cycles much more efficient and, of course, more successful.

question, "Do I have the decision-maker on my side?" Instead, ask yourself how well you know the distribution of influence at the customer firm and if the influential people are in your corner. Identifying the truly powerful—separating them from those who are merely wanna-bes—is a skill in which nearly all salespeople are weak. When you lose a sale at the last minute and take comfort in lamenting that "it was political," you are in fact trying to evade responsibility for not knowing who the true power players are and how influence flows in the buying company.

In short, when you have support from powerful people, you will find sales cycles much more efficient and, of course, more successful than if you persist in that endless search for the mythical decision-maker.

2. **The strength of your coach at the account.** A coach is someone who wants you to win the sale and is therefore willing to offer strategic and organizational information to help you toward that end. A coach does not have to be a powerful player within the customer organization, able to carry your torch for you. But she must understand her own company's business issues and organizational dynamics.

   Salespeople need to be clear-eyed in identifying their coaches, making certain they're not just friendly contacts—or worse, friendly enemies. Press yourself for hard evidence that your coach really wants you to win more than she wants your competitor to win. And the more complex the account, the more important it is to have a network of coaches. Nothing helps you shorten a sales cycle—win or lose—better than a good coach.

3. **Existing or past relationships between the two companies.** There are few greater advantages in selling than that of a positive past or current relationship with a prospect or customer. This must be a *business*

relationship, however—one that brings value to the customer, not merely a personal friendship between golfing buddies. But as any seasoned salesperson has learned, even a bad past can often be leveraged into a great opportunity—with an apology, when warranted, with corrective action, and with a demonstration of renewed commitment. It's where there is no relationship at all that a long and costly sales cycle is most likely.

4. **The depth of your business information about the target company.** Remember, executives are more inclined to buy from you based on what you know about their company and its business issues than based on what they know about you and your solution. Thus, your ability to win depends highly on your ability to demonstrate a compelling business fit with the account. You can do that only if you have taken the time to deeply understand the customer's business issues well beyond those that relate to your own product or service. Having a high degree of understanding of the customer's business greatly increases your probability of winning, and lowers the resources needed to do so.

5. **Changes taking place in the customer company.** One of my clients lost its third biggest customer when its salesperson failed to appreciate how his customer's shift from assembly line to cell manufacturing would profoundly change the way his customer used his product.

   This salesperson's experience is consistent with a general principle: change at a company makes the incumbent supplier vulnerable—and is the ideal time for the nonincumbent to launch an all-out assault. As a rule of thumb, if you're the outsider trying to crack an account, the more change taking place, the easier your job. But you must evaluate change well beyond those aspects of the customer's operations that relate solely to your solution.

THIS MUST BE A *BUSINESS* RELATIONSHIP, HOWEVER—ONE THAT BRINGS VALUE TO THE CUSTOMER, NOT MERELY A PERSONAL FRIENDSHIP BETWEEN GOLFING BUDDIES.

AS A RULE OF THUMB, IF YOU'RE THE OUTSIDER TRYING TO CRACK AN ACCOUNT, THE MORE CHANGE TAKING PLACE, THE EASIER YOUR JOB.

6. **The complexity of the decision process and your understanding of it.** Salespeople know how complex decision-making can be in their own companies, yet they often ignore that complexity in their accounts. Harry worked hard on a deal with a major beverage producer whose key contacts were located at eleven different sites. His boss had recommended walking away from the prospect in favor of more manageable targets, but, caught up in the emotional appeal of landing a big sale and betting on the strength of his solution, Harry spent several months pursuing the account anyway. Not surprisingly, he lost it—because he wasn't able to figure out the real decision process. The moral: The simpler and more centralized the buying decision, the less resource-intensive the sales cycle is likely to be.

   Similar issues arise when the buying company chooses to use a consultant or other third-party agent to manage the buying process. Such a situation should strongly influence any salesperson's decision as to how hard to pursue. Using third-party agents seems to be growing in popularity. It's pervasive in the software world. Consider how well you are pre-wired to the third party—or how well your competitors are. Doing so objectively can help you avoid a resource-intensive sales cycle that is lost before it starts.

7. **The customer's sense of urgency.** Is there a compelling event or set of circumstances that is causing the customer to make a purchase soon? Paul, another salesperson I know, was sucked into an expensive sales cycle only to find out ultimately that his contact was after information to justify to his own management why some of his department's functions should not be outsourced. He had no intention of buying anything. Because Paul failed to ask basic urgency questions, he unknowingly spent a lot of resources arming

> PAUL, ANOTHER SALESPERSON I KNOW, WAS SUCKED INTO AN EXPENSIVE SALES CYCLE ONLY TO FIND OUT ULTIMATELY THAT HIS CONTACT WAS AFTER INFORMATION TO JUSTIFY TO HIS OWN MANAGEMENT WHY SOME OF HIS DEPARTMENT'S FUNCTIONS SHOULD NOT BE OUTSOURCED.

his contact with information that helped him kill what was not a viable sales opportunity to begin with.

Knowing the customer's sense of urgency lets you assess the customer's level of pain. For a textbook example, think back to the issue of Y2K preparedness in the few years that preceded the year 2000. Clearly, this was a compelling event, one expected to lower the resources needed to win an account for a supplier of a Y2K-related solution. It's not enough to ask questions like, "When will you need delivery?" You must identify the specific urgent business driver.

8. **The strength of your solution relative to what the customer wants.** A strong solution is a plus, but it's less important than many other factors. Selling companies can become so enamored of their product or service that they genuinely believe, "If you build it they will come." Consider how many times you've lost a sale to a competitor who had a weaker solution or beaten a competitor who had a stronger one.

Having said this, I'm nevertheless the first to acknowledge that in many sales, scores of technical criteria must be met as a prerequisite to doing business. Such criteria are better viewed as "preopportunity assessment" criteria, which should be identified as early as possible in your discussions with a prospect to see if you should even be entering the game. For the Vendor, solution fit is usually where Opportunity Assessment stops; for the Business Resource, that's where it starts.

9. **Available budget dollars.** This criterion is important, but less so than you might think. In fact, being too absorbed with whether budget dollars exist for your product or service may indicate that you're selling at too low a level in the target company or selling into the wrong department, such as purchasing. Although the availability of funds can make your life easier, a strong preoccupation with budget is a Vendor trademark.

IT'S NOT ENOUGH TO ASK QUESTIONS LIKE, "WHEN WILL YOU NEED DELIVERY?" YOU MUST IDENTIFY THE SPECIFIC URGENT BUSINESS DRIVER.

SELLING COMPANIES CAN BECOME SO ENAMORED OF THEIR PRODUCT OR SERVICE THAT THEY GENUINELY BELIEVE, "IF YOU BUILD IT THEY WILL COME."

IF SENIOR MANAGEMENT CONSIDERS A PURCHASE IMPORTANT, THEY'LL FIND THE MONEY, WHETHER IT'S BUDGETED OR NOT. THE BUSINESS RESOURCE OPERATES ON THIS PREMISE.

OPPORTUNITY ASSESSMENT IS AMONG THE HIGHEST VALUE-CREATING ACTIVITIES A SALESPERSON PERFORMS IN THE REDEFINED WORLD OF SELLING. BECAUSE IT REQUIRES HIGH LEVELS OF BUSINESS ACUMEN AND JUDGMENT, IT CAN'T BE OFF-LOADED TO SOME OTHER CHANNEL.

If senior management considers a purchase important, they'll find the money, whether it's budgeted or not. The Business Resource operates on this premise.

Supplement these nine criteria with those that apply to your specific business. The result is a set of principles against which you can measure how efficiently you spend your time and your company's resources. You'll spend less time on accounts that are sure losers and sure winners, so you'll be able to devote far more of your precious selling time to accounts where your efforts can win or lose important business. You'll also become sharper at identifying accounts you would likely come to regret winning because of their poor fit with your company.

Opportunity Assessment is among the highest value-creating activities a salesperson performs in the redefined world of selling. Because it requires high levels of business acumen and judgment, it can't be off-loaded to some other channel, the way most other activities of the traditional salesperson can be.

Perhaps even more important than acumen and judgment, implementing Opportunity Assessment requires courage—courage to ask the needed questions and act on the information. It's not easy to suck it in and tell your own manager that you're going to walk away from or de-emphasize a particular opportunity. It's even harder to tell that to the customer. Just remember what it did for Rebecca in telling a prospect that her company had an obligation to remain healthy by investing in customer relationships that fit well with its own business philosophy.

Companies must fundamentally rethink how they segment customers. The timeworn approach of segmentation into small, medium, and large accounts has run its course. Instead, customers should be segmented and resourced by their value orientation. In other words, salespeople must develop the ability to assess what kind of relationship a customer wants and, in turn, assess their own company's ability to comply with that desired relationship in a way that yields *mutual* benefit. This is not easy, which is why I maintain that in selling's new business model, Opportunity Assessment will separate the pups from the big dogs.

In the past, the costs to a company of over-investing in a prospect or customer were either ignored or written off as a normal cost of doing business. Likewise, customers were remarkably forgiving of a supplier's underinvesting in them, no doubt reasoning that they probably couldn't get much better service and support elsewhere.

Overinvesting in, and underresourcing of, customers are phenomena of another era—known as the old era of selling.

OVERINVESTING IN, AND UNDERRESOURCING OF, CUSTOMERS ARE PHENOMENA OF ANOTHER ERA— KNOWN AS THE OLD ERA OF SELLING.

chapter 10

"Knowing it ain't the same as doing it."

—Old Hoosier saying

FROM TRAINING
TO TRANSFORMATION

THE SALES TRAINING MYTH

Tom, a seasoned salesperson, had just made a job change from an East Coast company to a Midwest company that had engaged my firm only two months earlier to transform its sales organization to the Business Resource level.

Coincidentally, a few months before Tom jumped ship, he and his colleagues on the sales team had been sent by their East Coast employer through one of the industry's popular strategic sales training seminars. At the time, Tom was elated to receive that training because he'd recognized the need to become more strategic in his sales approach. So he took to heart everything he was taught in the seminar, especially the stuff about selling to executives.

Yet, as he approached account after account in the months following the training, attempting to enlist the support of his contacts in securing a meeting with their senior management, he repeatedly found that they blocked him.

Tom related this experience to one of my firm's field implementation consultants as he was attempting to catch up with his new Midwest coworkers on the sales process they were learning from my company. Eager to see what was going wrong with his executive access attempts, Tom asked the consultant to conduct a joint call with him at the first opportunity.

Tom's chance came a short time later. Together they called on a contact at a large pharmaceutical company. At the close of the call, thinking he was following the playbook from the training program of his former East Coast employer, Tom suggested to his contact, Bill, a meeting with Bill's boss.

"Do you think this would be a good time to get [the executive] involved in this decision?" Tom asked casually.

Bill seemed to bristle a bit. "No, that won't be necessary," he replied.

This time, of course, Tom wasn't alone. The field implementation consultant was acting as Tom's "real-time coach," carrying a business card from Tom's company. He jumped in to reframe the request, saying:

> Bill, we recognize that you are the one who will make the decision. But I think you'll agree that this particular decision represents an initiative that would take the business relationship between our two companies to a whole new level, offering great potential for your company but also involving some additional risk. I think we'd both benefit if [the senior executive] were more familiar with the direction we're going together, so that he can more readily support us in the effort.

A CENTRAL TRUTH ABOUT ANY ATTEMPT TO EFFECT THE TRANSFORMATION OF A SALES FORCE TO THE BUSINESS RESOURCE LEVEL: SALES TRAINING ALONE CAN'T GET IT THERE.

Bill nodded in the affirmative and said, "That makes sense."

Tom's story is the rule, not the exception. It demonstrates a central truth about any attempt to effect the transformation of a sales force to the Business Resource level: Sales training alone can't get it there. As the old Hoosier saying goes, "Knowing it ain't the same as doing it."

The very same point came up in a conversation I had with a seatmate during the usual small talk on a cross-country flight. As it happened, this total-stranger-turned-confidant, Al, was a salesperson for a large, California-based technology company. Al told me that in the last nine months his employer had spent nearly $2 million on sales training.

"Did it do any good?" I asked.

His reply was blunt. "No, it was a waste of money. The content was good, the instructors were entertaining, and the materials were professional," Al said. "There were separate programs to teach managers and executives how to reinforce the training for the troops. And we bought the implementation software, too. But it wasn't long before everyone fell back into old habits, while senior management was under the illusion that the program was being implemented because they were getting their reports."

Rhetorically, I asked why no one said anything.

"Are you kidding?" he replied. "Our vice president of sales had just spent a few million dollars on this program. Who's going to stand up and say it was a wasted investment?"

Al's right. Many people aren't willing to stand up and proclaim that the emperor is naked—especially when it comes to sales training. But that's not the only problem. At most companies, virtually everyone who receives training that's intended to transform the sales force is either unaware of the training's lack of impact or is in denial about it. Half don't even realize that they're not implementing the training, and the other half won't admit they're not, lest it appear that they "didn't get it."

There's yet another dimension to this problem, an insidious dimension: Traditional sales training doesn't require sales reps to change. I maintain that this is the very reason so many salespeople embrace such training. And it seems everyone in the chain, from the reps to the execs, has a personal incentive to believe the training is working.

The truth is that upwards of 90 percent of learning from training is lost in one month, according to most studies. The upside to such a poor retention rate is that most of today's sales training is grounded in selling's old business model.

THERE'S YET ANOTHER DIMENSION TO THIS PROBLEM, AN INSIDIOUS DIMENSION: TRADITIONAL SALES TRAINING DOESN'T REQUIRE SALES REPS TO CHANGE. I MAINTAIN THAT THIS IS THE VERY REASON SO MANY SALESPEOPLE EMBRACE SUCH TRAINING.

SELLING HAS OPERATED UNDER THE SAME BASIC SET OF RULES FOR AS LONG AS ANY OF US CAN REMEMBER. AND SO HAS SALES TRAINING.

"CLASSROOM LEARNING DOESN'T WORK," SAYS RICK JUSTICE, SENIOR VICE PRESIDENT, WORLDWIDE FIELD OPERATIONS FOR CISCO SYSTEMS.

Selling has operated under the same basic set of rules for as long as any of us can remember. And so has sales training, with the seminar format. In recent years implementation software has been added to the mix. Still, the model has been essentially the same since sales training companies came into existence. They all have a program for this and a program for that.

"Classroom learning doesn't work," says Rick Justice, senior vice president, worldwide field operations for Cisco Systems, in the July 2000 issue of *Sales and Marketing Management*. Echoes Tom Kelly, Cisco's vice president for worldwide training, in the October 2000 *Fast Company*, "We were pulling thousands of people out of their jobs, out of contact with their customers, flying them to different locations and shutting them in classrooms for days at a time. It made no sense."

A study conducted at North Carolina State University and reported in *Fortune* concluded that "people can learn just as well with their PCs as they can by spending hours in the classroom." And a headline in the October 7, 1998, *USA Today* read, "Big lesson, billions wasted on job skills training. New studies show most learning happens outside a classroom."

A NEW PARADIGM FOR SELLING NEEDS A NEW PARADIGM FOR SALES TRAINING

In a previous career, I used to analyze metals through the lenses of high-powered electron microscopes, allowing my fellow metallurgists and me to see what was happening at a nearly atomic level. Viewing at such high magnification was an absolute prerequisite if the finished product—say, a turbine blade inside a jet engine—was to do its job.

It seems that almost every process in business today is undergoing a form of microscopic analysis at ever-higher magnification. The level of understanding—and control— of what is happening at the "atomic" level in manufacturing processes is staggering. From cars to carpets, virtually nothing in the production process is left to chance. The same is true in services; from French fries to finance, no detail is considered too small.

Not so in selling. If other processes were treated like the sales process, workers would be instructed to "buy some steel and make some cars," or "heat some oil and add potatoes," or "count the money and tell us how much we made." And the metallurgist would analyze the alloy, squinting at a sample held at arm's length.

Oddly, few companies display much interest in what happens in the sales process at the actual point of interaction between their sales reps and their customers. It's as if management is satisfied by viewing the scene through the wrong end of the microscope. And that's just the way salespeople like it. Some of the best selling that salespeople do is inside their own companies as they argue that they should be exempt from such scrutiny, claiming their value is relationship-based and can't be forced into the constraints of process.

Salespeople have always been the alchemists of business, each with his or her secret recipe for creating gold. What's more, most are careful to avoid sharing their recipes with other alchemists in the kingdom. After all, "As long as I'm creating more gold than my peers, I am the most highly favored alchemist in the king's eyes." There's no real malice in such attitudes—it's just the way things generally work. It's another one of selling's dirty little secrets.

Process is a bullet that salespeople won't be able to dodge much longer. Those who try—the ones who stubbornly or blindly think they can continue relying on their relationships for their value contribution—are in for a wake-up call. Fortunately, many salespeople are finally sobering up and embracing process.

Take Tom, from our earlier case, whose former employer invested heavily in his sales training. Tom's repeatedly unsuccessful attempts to reach executives is just one example out of millions. Not until Tom's process was "magnified"—that is, not until his actual inflections,

SOME OF THE BEST SELLING THAT SALESPEOPLE DO IS INSIDE THEIR OWN COMPANIES AS THEY ARGUE THAT THEY SHOULD BE EXEMPT FROM SUCH SCRUTINY, CLAIMING THEIR VALUE IS RELATIONSHIP-BASED AND CAN'T BE FORCED INTO THE CONSTRAINTS OF PROCESS.

tone, timing, and words were analyzed—was he able to see what was going wrong and fix it. Yet he was so sure he'd been implementing the process correctly.

From the words used to position a Knowledge Call to the rationale used in a decision to pursue an executive meeting, magnification of the process is desperately needed at all points throughout the sales process. And when one considers that the transformation from Vendor/Problem-Solver to Business Resource is so radical that it's like recoding one's DNA, the need for magnification of the process becomes even more critical.

WHEN ONE CONSIDERS THAT THE TRANSFORMATION FROM VENDOR/PROBLEM-SOLVER TO BUSINESS RESOURCE IS SO RADICAL THAT IT'S LIKE RECODING ONE'S DNA, THE NEED FOR MAGNIFICATION OF THE PROCESS BECOMES EVEN MORE CRITICAL.

SIX CONSIDERATIONS FOR TRANSFORMING YOUR SALES FORCE

Having now alienated most of my friends in the traditional sales training business, I give you a practical way to transform your sales force to the Business Resource level. Here are six recommendations to help you achieve that transformation:

1. **Start by asking yourself if you need a direct sales force at all.** Is a direct sales force your best channel to the market? If your customers' primary value requirement is low cost and ease of acquisition, you may want to rethink the value a direct sales force offers. When the sun comes up tomorrow morning, how dependent will your company's future be on the effectiveness of that sales force? If your sales force is supposed to be a primary vehicle for adding and creating value, then you clearly need one, and you most likely need it operating at the Business Resource level.

   In this case, you want to view sales as a core process in your company—no different from manufacturing or distribution or any other key process from which you derive significant competitive advantage and your customers derive significant value.

   On the other hand, if the main function of your salespeople is to communicate information about your company and its solutions, or to provide quasi service or engineering functions, it may be time to revisit your company's sales structure and consider replacing it, or at least complementing it, with other channels.

2. **Start with the right raw material.** A "salesy" personality and a lot of product smarts aren't enough, and may even be counterproductive. Just for starters, "salesy" people often have great difficulty moving from "tell" mode to "seek" mode, easily the most important step in the transformation to Business Resource.

Staff your sales force with people who demonstrate business acumen and organizational savvy. Has each candidate ever worked inside a corporate setting in a non-sales job? If not—and this may seem harsh—he or she should be presumed not to possess organizational savvy and should therefore be required to demonstrate otherwise, or at least a propensity for such, before being hired.

Does each candidate have the potential and desire to be executive credible? Don't think you can just hire Business Resource superstars from outside your company. This tactic is filled with holes. Unlike humorist Garrison Keillor's mythical Lake Wobegon, where "all the children are above average," the real world is made up of average people. So look first for potential—and desire—in your current ranks.

You may also want to expand your search to include others in the company who have little or no formal sales experience but whose skills and experience may agree with selling in this new selling environment.

3. **Make sure the new sales methodology you're considering is truly a process, is built around selling's new business model, and is providing concrete how-tos.** Most sales training gives its participants concepts, techniques, and even gimmicks to help them in one-to-one sales situations to persuade a prospect to choose the salesperson's product or service. These techniques won't

IF THE MAIN FUNCTION OF YOUR SALESPEOPLE IS TO COMMUNICATE INFORMATION ABOUT YOUR COMPANY AND ITS SOLUTIONS, OR TO PROVIDE QUASI SERVICE OR ENGINEERING FUNCTIONS, IT MAY BE TIME TO REVISIT YOUR COMPANY'S SALES STRUCTURE AND CONSIDER REPLACING IT, OR AT LEAST COMPLEMENTING IT, WITH OTHER CHANNELS.

do you much good in the new paradigm of selling. So consider closely whether the proposed training content has the potential to transform each sales candidate into a true Business Resource.

Webster's dictionary defines "process" as "a series of acts or changes, proceeding from one to the next." Does the sales methodology you're considering reflect a cohesive, repeatable process or merely a grab bag of ideas, stories, and concepts?

Does the proposed methodology address the complex sale? And does it teach process-related skills that fundamentally change the mindset of your sales force, right down to the very words each sales rep uses with customers and prospects?

4. **Construct your transformation model around e-learning combined with real-time coaching.** Should you drop the classroom entirely? Yes, if you view its primary value as that of "education" or "skills transfer." It's not that the classroom can't accomplish these results. It's just that it's too easy to get caught in the belief that simply because you spent all this time and money on flying everyone in for the multiday training event, you must have received a proportionate amount of value. The more money spent, the better the results, right?

Alternatively, if you view the primary value of the classroom session as a team-builder to help create momentum and set a clear direction for the transformation each salesperson is about to experience, then expectations are properly aligned with reality and the expense was worthwhile. Says Cisco's Tom Kelly in the October 2000 *Fast Company*:

> Most people are skeptical about learning that does not come in the form of classroom learning. You have to keep reminding them that the classroom retention rate is only about 25 percent after the first week and that from then on, people drop off significantly. The

BECAUSE YOU SPENT ALL THIS TIME AND MONEY ON FLYING EVERYONE IN FOR THE MULTIDAY TRAINING EVENT, YOU MUST HAVE RECEIVED A PROPORTIONATE AMOUNT OF VALUE. THE MORE MONEY SPENT, THE BETTER THE RESULTS, RIGHT?

main benefit of the classroom environment is human interaction—make new friends, strengthen relationships, that sort of thing. That's enormously important. But the classroom is not about acquiring knowledge. People need to accept that and stop clinging to a model that connects people but that doesn't teach people.

Compared with classroom training, e-learning achieves a similar level of effectiveness but also offers some value beyond simply saving time and money. Many studies indicate that e-learning can actually increase retention beyond that which is attainable in the classroom because it allows participants to work at their own pace and, to some extent, to use their ideal learning style.

E-LEARNING CAN ACTUALLY INCREASE RETENTION BEYOND THAT WHICH IS ATTAINABLE IN THE CLASSROOM.

However, now that you realize the significant difference between the traditional Vendor/Problem-Solver and the Business Resource, you can recognize that neither classroom training nor e-learning is anywhere near enough to effect the transformation to Business Resource. Real-time coaching is what's needed to complete the transformation. Such coaching is truly a radical departure from traditional training notions, but it is an essential step if salespeople are to internalize both the mindset and skill set required of a Business Resource.

Remember Tom, who fell back on his previous sales training when closing his call? He nearly blew it. But because he was accompanied by one of my firm's field implementation consultants—his real-time coach, who jumped in to reframe a critical question of Tom's—this experienced salesperson learned more in the final three minutes of that call than he had in three days in the classroom.

REAL-TIME COACHING HAS A "LEARNING DENSITY" INFINITELY GREATER THAN EITHER CLASSROOM WORK OR E-LEARNING.

His coach, of course, had been thoroughly steeped in all the critical details and nuances of executing the sales process. And that is only one example. Real-time coaching has a "learning density" infinitely greater than either classroom work or e-learning.

There are two different types of real-time coaching: strategy coaching and skills coaching. Both are equally important. Strategy coaching, as its name suggests, seeks to teach the *thought process* a salesperson uses while implementing a sales campaign. Strategy coaching does not require a direct customer interaction for the coaching to be effective.

Skills coaching, on the other hand, needs to occur during live sales calls with real customers if the learning is to have the proper effect in transforming the salesperson. Granted, some amount of skills coaching can be done with simulations, such as role-plays. But it's best to use simulations to *prepare for* live, real-time coaching. Skills coaching is what Tom's real-time coach was doing at Tom's pharmaceutical company account.

Skills coaching is a prerequisite to strategy coaching. My firm does not conduct strategy coaching with a salesperson until he or she has integrated enough of the skills coaching that we provide to (1) make us confident of the salesperson's assessment of a sales situation, and (2) convince us of the salesperson's ability to execute the strategy that we and this burgeoning Business Resource have codeveloped.

5. **Take a hard look at how your own internal culture creates barriers to the transformation you want to make.** Two barriers run neck and neck for top honors. First, many companies tell their sales force to develop long-term strategic business relationships with key customers, yet turn the screws for quarterly, monthly, or even daily numbers: paying for "x" while hoping for "y." The compensation plans in these companies usually reflect this disconnect, practically guaranteeing failure in any attempt to move to the Business Resource level.

The other leading barrier takes the form of a cultural overdependence on the product. From software companies whose cultures are driven by developers to manufacturing firms whose cultures are driven by

MANY COMPANIES TELL THEIR SALES FORCE TO DEVELOP LONG-TERM STRATEGIC BUSINESS RELATIONSHIPS WITH KEY CUSTOMERS, YET TURN THE SCREWS FOR QUARTERLY, MONTHLY, OR EVEN DAILY NUMBERS: PAYING FOR "X" WHILE HOPING FOR "Y."

engineers, the world's business landscape is filled with companies married to the notion, "If you build it, they will come." Unless this reliance on "the product" is shifted, it erects an insurmountable hurdle to the transformation from Vendor/Problem-Solver to Business Resource.

Because a company's cultural barriers tend to be deeply personal and political, few companies are able to diagnose and remedy them on their own. This is a good area to look to the outside for help.

6. **Expect that some of your people will not survive the transformation to Business Resource selling.** The kind of DNA-level change I am talking about does not agree with everyone. It can be traumatic for some. Not everyone will make it. If you are an executive or business owner, it is your responsibility to redeploy those who aren't cut out for it.

NEW BREED OF SALES MANAGER

Like the "salesman," the traditional sales manager is dying, too. But a new breed is springing up in its place.

Gone—if not now, soon—is the sales manager whose time is dedicated to *administrivia*: shuffling paper, auditing expense reports, writing fictional forecasts to show senior management just how well things are going in the field, enforcing sales quotas, and acting as the star closer.

For too many of these managers, mentoring salespeople ranks a distant priority, a when-I-can-get-to-it activity. Maybe that's not all bad, since most companies promote the superstar salesperson to sales manager, hoping to create clones. That tactic is as disastrous as it is pervasive, because the qualities that make a superstar salesperson are typically incompatible with the role of a superstar sales manager.

What does a sales manager at the level of Business Resource do? Here are seven responsibilities at the core of a sales manager's job description at a forward-thinking company.

GONE—IF NOT NOW, SOON—IS THE SALES MANAGER WHOSE TIME IS DEDICATED TO *ADMINISTRIVIA:* SHUFFLING PAPER, AUDITING EXPENSE REPORTS, WRITING FICTIONAL FORECASTS TO SHOW SENIOR MANAGEMENT JUST HOW WELL THINGS ARE GOING IN THE FIELD, ENFORCING SALES QUOTAS, AND ACTING AS THE STAR CLOSER.

1. **Remove internal obstacles.** Many corporate cultures are hostile toward their own sales force. Not deliberately or maliciously—it's just the way they are. This is almost always a result of one of the two cultural barriers discussed earlier: obsession with short-term results or overdependence on the product. To create a world-class sales force, you need to create a "friendly" environment in which they can succeed.

   A good sales manager needs polish and organizational savvy to fight the internal battles over account and territory assignments, deployment of technical support, compensation, channel conflicts, and cross-territory sales, to cite just a few examples. The manager's job is to free the sales force to do its job.

2. **Develop and implement a system of accountability.** We used to equate accountability in sales solely with numbers. The problem with that method is exemplified by a sales manager for a client of mine, a medical devices manufacturer. Kay told me she was going to promote one rep who was blowing the doors off the numbers. She also planned to put on notice another rep who was performing below quota. Having seen both at work, I was puzzled. I viewed the rep whom Kay was about to put on notice as more effective than the one designated for promotion.

   A closer look at the territories and the sales approaches of the two salespeople showed a discrepancy. The quota-buster had inherited a gold mine of a territory made up of large, producing accounts that required scant selling ability. The under-performer's territory was filled with promising, yet underdeveloped accounts.

   The supposed overachiever operated as a textbook Vendor-level salesperson. He possessed all the flash of the salesman archetype, yet he called on comfortable, low-level contacts using a basic approach of "Just checking in to see if there's anything going on." The supposed underachiever was clearly a Business Resource in the making. While not showing the same "salesy" style of her Vendor colleague, this individual demonstrated exceptional organizational savvy, operated in seek mode without even having to think about it, and was in the process of gaining executive meetings at a few of her accounts. A model accountability system measures the skills and strategic thinking associated with selling at the Business Resource level. Because if you have those, the numbers will follow.

3. **Reinforce a common sales methodology and sales message.** The rules and language, steps, and milestones of the sales process should be common throughout the sales organization. Too often, a sales force suffers from anarchy. A common methodology helps salespeople learn from each other and ensures consistency in how they position their company and its value message. Customers are rarely able to make objective judgments about what we sell; instead, they make judgments on how we sell.

   It's management's responsibility, not the sales force's, to develop your company's core positioning message and strategy for value creation. It's the responsibility of the sales force to implement them.

4. **Create account bases that make sense.** There are two things to consider here. First, salespeople usually want the solar system for their territory, while management prefers that they focus on the eastern half of Elm Street. Think of Kay, who was going to promote the wrong guy because of disparate territories. A sales manager must be familiar with the accounts to which the company is selling so that these accounts get distributed equitably. She must simultaneously fight off the constant toadying of salespeople who covet plum accounts. A sales manager with the best interests of

A MODEL ACCOUNTABILITY SYSTEM MEASURES THE SKILLS AND STRATEGIC THINKING ASSOCIATED WITH SELLING AT THE BUSINESS RESOURCE LEVEL. BECAUSE IF YOU HAVE THOSE, THE NUMBERS WILL FOLLOW.

the company in mind must not allow salespeople too many opportunities to cherry-pick.

At the same time, the sales manager needs to work against corporate America's unfortunate tendency to penalize the most successful salespeople by excessively cutting their territories or raising their quotas. Such practices add up to one more internal obstacle for the sales manager to navigate.

Second, and of significantly greater importance, today's sales manager must completely rethink how accounts are assigned to salespeople in the first place. As I discuss in Chapter 9, size-based criteria don't make much sense. Just because two customer companies are of similar size doesn't mean they are looking for the same kind of relationship with suppliers. The best way to segment accounts is by the value orientation of customers, which I touch on in Chapter 9 as well.

5. **Provide your sales force with market data, competitive data, and qualified leads.** Salespeople should not be expected to surf the Internet in search of prospects. This is a terrible under-utilization of the salesperson's talent. It is the responsibility of the selling company's management to provide reasonably qualified leads.

Sales managers must also take responsibility for arming their sales forces with good information about competitors. How else can we justify telling salespeople that in order to win, they have to take responsibility for making a competitor lose?

6. **Be a conduit for best practices.** As I allude to earlier, one of selling's dirty little secrets is that salespeople on the same team are not naturally disposed to help one another. They're driven more by gaining recognition than by receiving financial reward. When one cracks the code on selling a particular solution or acing a wily competitor, he's likely to share, at most, only part of

> JUST BECAUSE TWO CUSTOMER COMPANIES ARE OF SIMILAR SIZE DOESN'T MEAN THEY ARE LOOKING FOR THE SAME KIND OF RELATIONSHIP WITH SUPPLIERS.

> SALESPEOPLE SHOULD NOT BE EXPECTED TO SURF THE INTERNET IN SEARCH OF PROSPECTS.

what worked. There's no malice in this; usually it's not even conscious. This is just the nature of salespeople. They want to win, and that's always just a little harder when their peers know all the tricks they know.

A good sales manager can work closely with salespeople to extract and share best practices. One way is to hold regular best-practices meetings in which salespeople are required to contribute to the discussion in an environment that is both friendly and competitive, and gives salespeople the recognition they crave for making such contributions.

7. **Take responsibility for mentoring and personal development**. Do you have what it takes to mentor others? Too often, superstars promoted to sales manager don't mentor or coach at all—they simply *take over* the sale. The consummate manager is able to draw out a salesperson's own ability to develop and execute the sales strategy. A great manager is able to draw out the abilities of his or her entire sales force and is able to ensure that they are all implementing the same process. Moreover, sales managers must coach, not only on sales *strategy*, which can be done in the office and sometimes even with groups of salespeople, but on sales *skills*, too, which can be done only in the field with real customers.

What a disaster it can be to promote the superstar salesperson to manager. But I've also known many sales superstars who went on to become highly effective sales managers. When it's time to promote to management, superstar status should neither pose an automatic barrier nor offer a free ride. What it takes is the willingness and the ability on the part of a sales manager to spend every day attending to these seven tasks. They are the secret to successful sales management in the new era of selling.

TOO OFTEN, SUPERSTARS PROMOTED TO SALES MANAGER DON'T MENTOR OR COACH AT ALL—THEY SIMPLY *TAKE OVER* THE SALE.

A Note to Executives and Business Owners

Nothing contributes more to the success or failure of the transformation of your company's sales force than your own leadership. Nothing! You can approve the funding and say all the right words at the kickoff, then go on to other things believing that you've done your part. Don't kid yourself. You, as a senior executive, can delegate management of the project, but you can't delegate leadership of the transformation.

You know about leadership, so lead this transformation as you would any other mission-critical initiative. Specifically, here are your marching orders, and there are only three:

> YOU, AS A SENIOR EXECUTIVE, CAN DELEGATE MANAGEMENT OF THE PROJECT, BUT YOU CAN'T DELEGATE LEADERSHIP OF THE TRANSFORMATION.

1. **Walk the talk.** Actively participate in the process. Attend group sessions and get in the field together with the salespeople as co-implementor of the process with the salesperson, not as the heavyweight from headquarters paraded in to do his heavyweight stuff. (Nobody—the customer, the salesperson, or you—really knows what that is, anyhow.) Take your cues from the salesperson as to what specifically she needs you to do. At the same time, hold her feet to the fire, insisting that she tell you where she is in the sales process, what the business issues and organizational dynamics are, and what result she's looking to achieve in the call. Never let the salesperson get away with taking you in simply to introduce you.

    Conduct a few Knowledge Calls with salespeople. Only then are you able to feel, up close and personal, the heartbeat of the process and, in doing so, gain untold credibility with the troops. When you attend a Business Presentation, remember that it's the salesperson's meeting, not yours. You may even need to remind the salesperson of that. Salespeople are often intimidated by your presence. You're there to reinforce and support what the salesperson says. That way the customer sees the salesperson as a resource in your company—and one with clout.

2. **Get unanimous commitment from the senior management team.** Simply put, either get the unqualified commitment of your management team or reconsider attempting the transformation until circumstances change, or until you change those circumstances. To hope that a key member of the team will eventually "come on board" is a recipe for failure.

   You and the rest of your team must create a strong sense of urgency around the transformation. Not the rah-rah kind of urgency but the house-is-on-fire kind. Salespeople must view the transformation as critical to the company's very survival, not as an opportunity to merely acquire a few new skills. This sense of urgency also helps to ease the removal of the many cultural, procedural, and bureaucratic hurdles inevitably lining the path.

3. **Transform your own thinking from "numbers" alone to "successful execution of a sound process."** I've seen more would-be-successful transformation projects fail in the long run because management loses its patience with process and falls back to its comfort zone—the numbers. As an absolute prerequisite, you must have total confidence in the sales process you're embracing to effect the transformation. Never use the project to test whether or not a chosen sales process works in your environment, i.e., "Let's try the process on a few accounts. If we close business, then it must be a good process." If you show unwavering belief in the process and the people associated with the transformation project, you will achieve the desired end.

   It's understandable that the numbers have historically been the only measure of the performance of the sales team. There was really no other way to assess the output of their "special art." Now there is. As process

TO HOPE THAT A KEY MEMBER OF THE TEAM WILL EVENTUALLY "COME ON BOARD" IS A RECIPE FOR FAILURE.

YOU AND THE REST OF YOUR TEAM MUST CREATE A STRONG SENSE OF URGENCY AROUND THE TRANSFORMATION. NOT THE RAH-RAH KIND OF URGENCY BUT THE HOUSE-IS-ON-FIRE KIND.

replaces artistry in professional selling, metrics can be established to gauge how effectively the process is being implemented by each salesperson.

Unlike measuring by the numbers, which yields a lagging indicator of success, being able to transform your thinking will yield a predictor of success. As such, it affords you the ability to get a read on a salesperson even before he or she starts succeeding—or failing to succeed—in the production of numbers.

THE WORLD-CLASS SALESPERSON IN THE NEW ERA OF SELLING

It's not just a matter of changes to the rules of the game we call selling—it's a different game being played. Soon, the lights over the old playing field will go dark, and the weeds will grow tall and overtake the grass. If you're still swinging the bat and running the bases in the dark on the old field, it's only a matter of time before you're beaned by the ball or strangled by the weeds.

The more homers you hit or strikeouts you pitched throughout your career, the more likely you are to cling to the old game. After all, you were a world-class player.

But there's room—lots of room—for world-class players in the new game of selling. I know many. Some were sales rookies, having spent only a season or so playing the old game. But many, many others made the transformation after twenty or more seasons in the old league.

The superstar salespeople in the new era of selling all have one thing in common: They've let go of the old game. They've accepted that they're not immune to the forces of economic and technological change, clinging stubbornly to their old, comfortable, Vendor/Problem-Solver practices. They've stopped arguing that they are some sort of special case whose value contribution is derived from their unique relationship skills or technical prowess. They've given up the fight against sales process.

The world-class salespeople in the new era of selling have made the personal decision to redefine themselves—

BUT THERE'S ROOM—LOTS OF ROOM—FOR WORLD-CLASS PLAYERS IN THE NEW GAME OF SELLING. I KNOW MANY. SOME WERE SALES ROOKIES, HAVING SPENT ONLY A SEASON OR SO PLAYING THE OLD GAME. BUT MANY, MANY OTHERS MADE THE TRANSFORMATION AFTER TWENTY OR MORE SEASONS IN THE OLD LEAGUE.

to recode their DNA, as it were—so that each can become a world-class Business Resource.

And based on my conversations with many of them, "It only hurts for a little while."

Index

access letters, 106–12, 113

accountability, 190–91

account bases, 191–92

adventure, 23–24

alignment. *See* business fit; philosophical alignment

The Art of War (Sun Tzu), 145–46, 150

Atlanta, as Olympics site, 141–42

attitude, 79–81

auction economy, on the Web, 5, 8–9

automotive industry, 62

Barnes, Jhane, 157

best practices, sharing of, 192–93

Britten, Kent, 9

B-to-B (business-to-business) commerce, on the Web, 9

business fit, 5, 85–86, 93, 129, 133

    See also philosophical alignment

Business Presentations, 123–40

    achieving success with, 137–39

    attendees at, 130–31

    and business fit, 129

    for confirming vs. educating/selling, 127–28, 137–38

    content of, 132–36

    vs. discussion, 125–26

    executive credibility resulting from, 139–40

    vs. executive dialogues, 125

    managing the meeting vs. giving a speech, 131, 137

    media for, 136–37

    vs. proposals, 16–17, 24, 127–28

    rehearsing, 139

    in sales campaigns, 128

    sample of, 134–35

    timing of/opportunities for, 128–30

    transitions during, 138–39

    wiggle words during, 138

business profile of customer, 84

Business Resource, 13–25

    and adventure, 23–24

    and Business Presentations vs. proposals, 16–17, 24 (*see also* Business Presentations)

    and business vs. personal relationship building, 20

    and comfort zones, 23

    and creating vs. fulfilling opportunities, 18–19

    and customer business knowledge vs. product knowledge, 21, 24 (*see also* customer's business, understanding of)

    customer perception of salesperson's value, 14–15

    and executive credibility vs. comfortable contacts, 5, 16

    and executives, getting to, 24 (*see also* executive meetings)

    and how vs. what you sell, 13–14

    and opportunity assessment vs. gut feel, 17, 24 (*see also* opportunity assessment)

    and organizational savvy vs. looking for the decision-maker, 15–16, 24 (*see also* organizational savvy)

    and owning the customer vs. sales activity, 18

    and positioning, 24 (*see also* positioning)

    and seek vs. tell mode, 19–20, 24 (*see also* seek mode)

    and steering the sales campaign, 21–22

    and strategy/positioning vs. competing, 19

    transformation to, 24 (*see also* transformation)

    Vendor/Problem-Solver vs., 14–15

    and winning vs. losing a deal, response to, 22

Business Week, 6–7

buying. *See* purchasing

change, fear of, xv, 23

Clinton, Bill, 153, 155

Close, Wendy, 73

coaches, 33, 34–35, 68, 88, 172

coaching, real-time, 187–88

comfort zones, 23

commitment, mutual, 94–95

communications technology, 6–7
    See also Internet

compatibility, company-to-company, 95–96

Competitive Engagement, 145–53, 154, 157

computers/bandwidth, as free, 5–8

confidentiality, 40, 45

contacts
    dialogues with, 117–20
    executive meetings via, 112, 114–17
    influence of, 115
    for Knowledge Calls, 33–35
    and management levels, 114–15
    personal relationships with, 114
    rejection from, 116–17
    wording requests to, 115–16

core competency focus, 169–70

Crocodile Dundee, 147

culture of a company, 171, 188–89, 190

curiosity, 27–28, 87

customers
    attitude toward, 171
    knowledgeable, 7–8, 9, 73

customer's business, understanding of, 73–90
    and attitude, 79–81
    in Business Presentations, 132
    as a competitive weapon, 78–79
    and controlling the sales situation, 82–83
    and customer needs, 81–82
    and the Knowledge Call, 86–87 (*see also* Knowledge Calls)
    mileage from, 90 (*see also* Business Presentations)
    outline for pursuing, 83–86
    and the Problem-Solver approach, 75–76
    and product-focused salespeople, 74
    vs. product knowledge, 21, 24
    relevance of, 76–78
    sources of information, 79–80, 83 (*see also* Knowledge Calls)

sufficient knowledge, 87–88
    targets for, 88–90

decision-makers, finding, vs. organizational savvy, 15–16, 24, 51–53, 71

demand creation, 5, 12, 97, 119–20

DeVincentis, John, 3, 12

dialogues with contacts, 117–20

direct engagement with competitors, 146–48

drivers, key, of the customer, 84–85

Drucker, Peter, 58

Economist, 1, 2–3

Einstein, Albert, 144

e-learning, 186–87

executive credibility, 139–40

executive meetings, 91–121
    and access letters, 106–12, 113
    arranging, 120
    and the Business Resource vs. Vendor mindset, 104–5
    choosing executives to approach, 103–4
    vs. comfortable contacts, 5, 16
    and company-to-company compatibility, verifying, 95–96
    via contacts, 112, 114–17
    vs. decision-maker pursuits, 105–6
    dialogues to win access to, 117–20
    and executive assistants, 105–6
    and executives' desire to see salespeople, 91–93, 120–21
    and Knowledge Calls, 34–35, 89–90, 108
    and mutual commitment, establishing, 94–95
    objections to, 92–93
    opportunities for, 99–102
    purpose of, 93–94
    rejection from contacts to request for, 116–17
    timing of, 96–97
    when to stay away from, 97–99
    wording of requests for, 115–16

executives
    attitude toward vendors, 171

leadership of, 194–96
See also executive credibility; executive
        meetings
expertise, 65–66

fear of change, xiii, 23
fear of speaking before an audience, 126
flip charts, 136–37
Ford, 8
Fortune
    on Atlanta as Olympics site, 141–42
    on customer knowledge, 9
    on the death of the vendor, 4
    on the RFQ process, 11
    on Web auctions, 8–9

Gardner, Bill, 4
gatekeepers, 33–34, 68, 88–89, 97–98
Gault, Stanley, 159
GM, 8
Grove, Andy, 7, 12, 91, 145

hiring a sales force, 185
Holden, Jim, 146
House, Pat, 12

indirect engagement with competitors, 148–53,
        154
influence
    of contacts, 115
    signs of, 68–71
    sources of, 64–66
    vs. title, 60–64, 103–4
    tools for identifying, 67–68
information
    gathering of, vs. Knowledge Calls,
        28–31
    overload of, 144, 145
    sharing of, 169
    See also Knowledge Calls
initial cost, 170
initiatives/priorities of customer, 85
Internet, 5–11

Justice, Rick, 182

Kelly, Tom, 182, 186–87
Knowledge Calls, 28–49
    conducting, 42–49
    and confidentiality, 40, 45
    contacts for, 33–35
    controlling logistics of, 39–41
    customer business knowledge via, 86–87
    and executive meetings, 34–35, 89–90, 108
    vs. information-gathering, 28–31
    listening during, 45–46
    lunch meetings, 40
    next step following, 47–48
    note taking during, 47
    vs. other sales calls, 31–33
    and outline for pursuing information, 83–86
    by phone, 48–49
    positioning of/requests for, 32, 35–39, 43–45
    preparing for, 41–42
    questions in, 46–47, 86–87
    silence during, 46
    tone of, 42–43
    warm-up during, 43, 86

Lank, Avrum, 4
Loman, Willy (fictional character), xv, xvi–xviii

manager, new breed of, 189–93
marketing visibility, 168
Matlow, Dave, xv–xvi
Meakem, Glen, 11
mentoring, 189, 193
Miller, Avram, 57–58

natural gas, 103–4
North Carolina State University, 182

opportunities
    for approaching executives, 99–102
    for Business Presentations, 128–30
    creating vs. fulfilling, 18–19, 97
    See also opportunity assessment

opportunity assessment, 159–77
    and budget, 175–76
    and business information, depth of, 173
    and changes within customer company, 173
    and coaches, 172
    and complexity of decision process, 174
    and existing/past relationships, 172–73
    good deals/relationships, 163–66
    vs. gut feeling, 17, 24, 160
    marketing visibility, 168
    philosophical fit, 169–71
    profitability, 167
    and qualification of sales potential, 160–62
    quality of potential business relationship,
        168–71
    quality of specific sales opportunity, 167–68
    resources needed for success, 171–77
    and strength of solution, 175
    and support from powerful people, 171–72
    and urgency, customer's sense of, 174–75
    walking away, 159
    and wasted time/effort, 162–63
organizational charts, 67, 68
organizational savvy, 5, 51–71
    vs. finding the decision-maker, 15–16, 24,
        51–53, 71
    importance of, 53–56
    and influence, signs of, 68–71
    and influence, sources of, 64–66
    and influence, tools for identifying, 67–68
    and influence vs. title, 60–64
    and politics/power, 52, 57–60, 66, 71
    in practice, 66
    and profiles of key players, 67–68
    salespeople as lacking, 56–57
owning the customer vs. sales activity, 18

Payne, Billy, 141–42
personality of a company, 171
philosophical alignment, 5, 95–96, 169–71
    See also business fit
politics, corporate, 52, 57–60, 66, 71
politics, national, 59–62, 64

positioning, 5, 24, 141–58
    and access to executives, 102
    in Business Presentations, 132–33
    vs. competing, 19
    and Competitive Engagement, 145–53, 154,
        157
    importance of, 144–45
    of Knowledge Calls, 32, 35–39, 43–45
    putting competitors on the defensive, 153,
        155–56
    word choice in, 156–58
power. See influence; politics, corporate
PowerPoint, 136
pragmatic positioning. See positioning
price buyer, 170
pricing, 2–3
process
    magnification of, 183–84
    vs. numbers, 195–96
    training as, 185–86
product superiority, 1–2
profiles of customers, 84
profiles of key players, 67–68
profitability, 167
public speaking, fear of, 126
purchasing
    decisions, reasons for, 144–45
    philosophy of, 170–71
    strategic, 5, 10–11

Rackham, Neil, 3, 12
Raiders of the Lost Ark, 149
relationship building, 4, 7, 20
Request for Proposal (RFP), 150–51
Request for Quotation (RFQ) process, 10–11
retail industry, large, 62
RFP (Request for Proposal), 150–51
RFQ (Request for Quotation) process, 10–11
Rite Aid drug stores, 8
Roberts, George, 2–3

sales calls, cost of, 11
sales campaign, steering, 21–22

sales force, 3, 184–85
sales manager, new breed of, 189–93
salesmanship, and the death of the vendor, 2
Sales & Marketing Management, 3, 12, 74
seek mode
    and curiosity, 27–28
    vs. tell mode, 5, 19–20, 24, 50
    See also Knowledge Calls
selling, and the death of the vendor, 4–5
Siebel, Thomas, 12
simplicity, 144, 174
skills coaching, 188, 193
strategic purchasing, 5, 10–11
strategy. *See* positioning
strategy coaching, 188, 193
Sun Tzu, 27
    The Art of War, 145–46, 150

technology, 3
    See also Internet
territories, 191–92
Thatcher, Margaret, 71
timing, 96–97
title vs. influence, 60–64
total cost of ownership, 170
training
    e-learning, 186–87
    myth of, 179–82
    new paradigm for, 182–84
    as a process, 185–86
    real-time coaching, 187–88
transformation, 24, 179–97
    and accountability, 190–91
    and account bases/territories, 191–92
    and coaching, real-time, 187–88
    and a common methodology, 191
    considerations for, 184–89
    and e-learning, 186–87
    and executive leadership of, 194–96
    and hiring a sales force, 185
    internal culture as barrier to, 188–89, 190
    and mentoring, 189, 193
    and need for direct sales force, 184–85
    and process, magnification of, 183–84
    and process vs. numbers, 195–96
    and providing sales force with data/leads, 192
    and the sales manager, new breed of, 189–93
    and salespeople who are unable to change, 189
    sales training, new paradigm for, 182–84
    and the sales training myth, 179–82
    and sharing of best practices, 192–93
    and training as a process, 185–86
    and world-class salespeople, 196–97

unit price, 170
USA Today, 157, 182

value buyer, 170
value contribution, 65
vendor, death of
    and the Internet, 5–11
    and pricing, 2–3
    and product superiority, 1–2
    sales force, shrinkage of, 3
    and salesmanship, 2
    and selling, 4–5
    and technology, 3
von Hildebrand, Dietrich, 144

Wall Street Journal
    on B-to-B commerce, 9
    on communications technology, 7
    on the Internet, 8, 9
    on presentations, 126
Wal-Mart, 7
WDM technology, 6–7
Web, 5–11
word choice
    during Business Presentations, 138
    in positioning, 156–58
    in requests for executive meetings, 115–16

Young, Andy, 141–42